CW00894066

Give Your Child a Better Start

Michael Howe is the author of many titles
of which the most recent are:

THE ORIGINS OF EXCEPTIONAL ABILITIES
SENSE AND NONSENSE ABOUT HOTHOUSE CHILDREN
ENCOURAGING THE DEVELOPMENT OF EXCEPTIONAL SKILLS AND
TALENTS

Give Your Child a Better Start

How To Encourage Early Learning

MICHAEL HOWE and HARRIET GRIFFEY

MICHAEL JOSEPH · LONDON

MICHAEL JOSEPH LTD

Published by the Penguin Group
27 Wrights Lane, London W8 5TZ
Viking Penguin Inc., 375 Hudson Street, New York, New York 10014, USA
Penguin Books Australia Ltd, Ringwood, Victoria, Australia
Penguin Books Canada Ltd, 10 Alcorn Avenue, Toronto, Ontario, Canada M4V 3B2
Penguin Books (NZ) Ltd, 182–190 Wairau Road, Auckland 10, New Zealand

Penguin Books Ltd, Registered Offices: Harmondsworth, Middlesex, England

First published in Great Britain August 1994
Second impression October 1994

Copyright © Michael Howe and Harriet Griffey 1994

Filmset by Datix International Limited, Bungay, Suffolk
Printed in England by Clays Ltd, St Ives plc
Set in 12/14pt Monophoto Garamond

ISBN 0 7181 3727 2

The moral right of the authors has been asserted

Contents

For Josh (HG)
and for Nick and Lucy (MH)

Acknowledgements

The authors are grateful to a number of individuals for giving help and advice or commenting on earlier drafts of the chapters. We are especially indebted to Nick Moon, who made a large number of valuable suggestions, and we would also like to thank Stuart Biddle, Kim and Clare Economides, Janice Kay, Alan Slater, Paul and Julie Webley, and Brian and Sadie Young.

1 | A Better Start

Like most parents who care about their children's futures, you know how important it is for your youngsters to get off to a good start in life. You are willing to do your best on their behalf. You want your children to be lively and happy, to do well at school, to enjoy fulfilling lives and success at their chosen careers. You are only too aware how frustrating adult life can be for those who leave school without the skills and capabilities that young people need today in order to get what they want from our complicated world. You hope that your children will grow up to be intelligent, imaginative, confident, and well-educated people.

The purpose of this book is to help you help make that happen. To do so, two crucial but unappreciated facts about early childhood need to be understood.

Fact one: to a far greater extent than most parents realize, whether a child becomes a capable and intelligent young person depends not just on chance, luck or genetic inheritance, but on the use parents make of early opportunities to learn – opportunities which are available to all parents. Everyday activities which parents engage in with their babies and young children have a truly enormous influence on a young child's progress and her ability to learn.

Fact two: it is entirely possible for every parent to provide the kind of early start that maximizes the chances that child will grow up capable, imaginative, and intelligent.

You may think that you cannot 'teach' your child, but the fact is that you certainly can and, what is more, you already do. Whenever you play with your baby, or when you and your child respond to each other or enjoy a game together, you are being an effective teacher, even though you may not be aware of it. A great deal of early learning takes place at home without parents being at all deliberate about teaching, or even conscious that it is happening. *You do not need to have any special skills in order to be effective at encouraging your child to learn.*

This book introduces some pleasurable new activities that you can share with your child, and helps you to find ways of getting the most out of the activities you already enjoy. No enormous efforts or painful sacrifices are necessary. Far from imposing a burden on either parent or child, the everyday games and activities described in this book will add to your own fun as well as helping your child to make better progress as a young learner.

LEARNING IN THE FAMILY

Some parents are too ready to assume that experts always know best and that out-of-home learning facilities are superior to what they themselves can provide. So far as early learning is concerned, that is simply not true. It is important to realize that the child's own home provides a superb setting for learning, with the special advantage that at home is it likely that there will be lots of opportunities for one-to-one interaction between the child and a caring adult person.

That does not mean that parents have to stay at home all the time. This is not a practical possibility for many working parents, and research has shown that the overall amount of time that parent and child spend together is not necessarily that important. What *is* essential is that parents make a real effort to ensure that there is *some* time each day when a child can count on having a parent's more or less undivided attention. It doesn't matter if these sessions are sometimes very short. Even a five minute period can provide learning opportunities, though it is preferable to have longer.

Opportunities for parent and child to spend time doing things together have special benefits in the crucial area of language development. Mastering language is particularly important because, as well as being the key to communicating with other people, it opens up all kinds of new possibilities for the young learner, significantly enlarging the child's capacity to think and understand.

In helping a child's language development, parents have two huge advantages. Not only are they able to give their full attention to their own child, they are also the people who know their child best. That is not to deny that preschool facilities outside the home, such as day nurseries, playgroups, kindergartens and playschools, are often helpful for stimulating early learning. But their effectiveness is restricted by the fact that these learning environments cannot provide the close individual attention that promotes the development of language and thinking. And because young children can find it quite stressful to be in a large, perhaps noisy group of other people, they may find it hard to relax and concentrate on what they are doing. Preschool facilities can complement the learning experiences a child enjoys at home, but they cannot substitute for them.

Psychologists Barbara Tizard and Martin Hughes have pointed out that because of the shared experiences parents and children have at home, it is often much easier for a parent than for a teacher to understand what a child is trying to say. Because of this, the parent is best placed to help the child make sense of new events by linking them with what is already familiar, something which happens quite naturally as you talk and listen to your child.

Parents have the further advantage of knowing that the child's own family life is filled with experiences that are meaningful and interesting for her because they play a part in the practical business of daily living. Within the home the family's meals are planned, cooked and cleared away, clothes are washed and ironed, babies are looked after, pets are tended, gardens are cultivated, telephone calls are made, letters are written, bills are paid, shopping is planned, and so on. Many of the activities that parents and children can share are ones that are linked to these practical events. So talking about them is easy and natural. Experiences such as helping with the cooking, making a shopping list, laying the table, caring for a baby or the pet cat, all help promote learning because they are intrinsically interesting and purposeful for the child. There is a real point and a reason for doing these activities, so they readily gain children's attention.

Because they have these powerful advantages, with a little assistance even the least confident parents who are convinced they possess no teaching skills can be highly effective at helping their own children to learn. And indeed research has confirmed that the activities parents provide for their growing child do have an enormous influence on both early progress and later achievements. In a few instances, parents have organized themselves in order to capitalize on this fact; for example, an American 'Parents as Teachers' scheme launched in Missouri during the 1980s has proved very successful, with one to three year olds showing above-average gains in language, conceptual ability and social skills.

It is not that schools do not matter. Nurseries, play-schools, daycare and other facilities can and do make a positive contribution to learning. They bring other benefits as well, not the least of which is that of giving exhausted parents some 'time off' from the constant demands of energetic toddlers. Even the most dedicated parents need to get away from their children at times. But as a source of opportunities for young children to make progress, especially at those skills that depend on or contribute to language development, the family is where the greatest scope lies. Parents who are keen to ensure their children get a good start early in life will be surprised and delighted to discover just how much can be achieved at home.

It is unfortunate that parents have not been given more encouragement to help their young children learn. Many young adults may find life a struggle simply because they were not given a good start in the early years. In most cases the problem is not that their parents did not care. Many say that they would have liked to do more to help their child make progress, but were not at all sure how best to achieve this. Sadly, they were not able to find the practical help they needed.

This book is designed to remedy that situation. It shows parents and others how to introduce a variety of everyday activities that will make a real difference to children, and give them a better start in learning to learn. It is mostly concerned with practical ways of helping a young child to learn; with down-to-earth information and suggestions, showing you how to encourage this.

THE PARENT AS A GUIDE

Becoming really effective at encouraging your child to learn is much easier than you think. It does not mean devoting an absurd amount of time to helping your child, and you will not have to engage in any activities that you and your child don't both enjoy. The kinds of learning activities which are most effective with young children rarely involve conventional instruction. You will find that most of the activities that work best are ones that involve parent and child playing games, having fun, doing things together and getting to know each other better. There is no pressure involved for either parent or child.

When parents are able to give a child their full attention, each can respond to the other. They share experiences, play, and begin to enjoy having two-way dialogues. All this starts to happen well before the child learns to talk, by introducing activities that involve doing things together, taking turns and having fun. Play is central to successful early learning. Through play, parents guide their child towards experiences that help them to make genuine progress.

In many ways 'guiding' is a much better word than 'teaching' for describing the kinds of activities parents can do best. At its simplest, guiding is just a matter of saying 'Look at this!' or 'Watch out for that!' or 'Hey, there's something really interesting!'. An effective guide is simply drawing attention to those aspects of a new or unfamiliar experience that matter, ones that are especially interesting or significant.

In order to be a good guide you will need to consider how the world must appear from the child's point of view, and what her needs and limitations are. You will not always succeed of course, but with a bit of effort much of the time you will. You will also need to remember that a guide's role is to help create opportunities for the child to learn. Over time you will learn how to do this more effectively, but the chances are that you are already more skilled at it than you think. In all probability you already make a point of drawing your child's attention to interesting objects and events. Whenever you do that, you are giving her the basis of a new learning experience.

Young humans are avid learners and eager to explore. Fortunately, most children's everyday lives are filled with stimulating events that provide potential learning opportunities. Learning always works best as a process in which the child actively participates, for children do not just absorb knowledge passively. However interesting and stimulating the world is, children do need a great deal of help in order to make sense of it. For the very young the world can sometimes seem *too* stimulating, and too confusing to be an ideal learning environment, which is why a parent needs to be a sensitive guide, mindful of the child's perspective.

Imagine yourself in a strange country. There is a great deal happening, but you find it impossible to understand what is going on or to make sense of what people are saying. The problem is not that it isn't stimulating or interesting, or that you are not keen to learn, but that there is so much that is totally unfamiliar. Because of that you find it frustratingly difficult to understand what is going on. Things are not entirely different for a young child. A baby may fail to learn from all the exciting things that are happening around her, as she finds them simply bewildering. Although she is a keen problem solver and a curious seeker of knowledge, there is simply too much going on and too many strange experiences for her to absorb them all.

What a baby requires is someone who can patiently help her begin to make sense of the everyday world, perhaps by directing attention to things which are especially important for her, one at a time. A guide who can do this will make things less confusing, and help the baby to structure new experiences by concentrating on that which really matters to her. For babies and young children it is especially important for the guide to be someone whose attention can be counted upon, who is aware of the child's limitations and is willing to try to see how the world must appear through a child's eyes.

Even the most enjoyable learning games are worthless unless the child is enthusiastic about playing them. Since a young child's attention span can be very short, you will have to be prepared to abandon a particular activity when your child becomes bored, tired or distracted. And bear in mind that it is never wise to criticize a young child's efforts to learn. That does no good at all.

AVOIDING UNREALISTIC EXPECTATIONS

Most parents today realize that children who are encouraged and given plenty of opportunities for learning basic skills tend to do well at school. But equally they are often concerned, and reasonably so, about the possibility that over-enthusiasm for early learning can have negative effects. The fear is that too much emphasis on accelerated learning will lead to a young child being 'pushed' or pressurized to succeed, that the child will be subjected to over-intensive 'hothouse' training. Many parents worry that while such a regime may succeed in forcing rapid growth in knowledge and mental skills, it will succeed at a heavy cost. Their concern is that the child will be denied the many varied experiences that provide fun, friendship and that healthy emotional development we want for our children.

These worries are shared by many. They are certainly justified. Occasionally a parent who has set out to make a child into a prodigy of learning has succeeded, as James Mill did with his son John Stuart Mill, but such attempts have usually ended in failure, sometimes with disastrous consequences for the child. Too much pressure can indeed be harmful: unrealistic parental expectations are sometimes crippling. There is nothing wrong with encouraging high aspirations, but no child likes to be made to feel he or she is always being tested. Although it is not always easy to draw a clear line between encouraging children and pushing them, it is important to keep the distinction in mind. When we conducted research into the family backgrounds of successful young musicians (see Chapter 14) we consistently encountered families who gave plenty of encouragement to their children yet avoided too much pressure to succeed.

You can be sure that none of the learning activities described here will, in themselves, place any kind of pressure on a young child. It is always sensible to be alert to that possibility, but don't forget that children are curious and have healthy appetites for learning. Parents are not pushing their children when they give them opportunities to explore and discover new things.

HOW MUCH TIME DO YOU NEED TO SPEND?

How long do parents need to devote to learning activities with their child, in order to make a real difference? It is an important question, but there is no simple answer, because there are so many different factors to take into account. In any case it is not the sheer amount of time that parent and child spend in the same room that is crucial: what is much more important is the amount of time spent doing things *together*. The time that goes into any kind of shared activity which involves playing games together, or any kind of dialogue or interaction that includes give and take or taking turns, is likely to be especially valuable as far as a child's learning is concerned.

Many toddlers would not expect to have the more or less undivided attention of an adult for as much as twenty minutes a day. A child who has around forty minutes of this kind of daily attention will be getting an above average share of good learning opportunities. Parents should regard around forty minutes as a reasonable minimum. An hour would be better, preferably divided into a number of smaller chunks.

With young babies, finding this amount of time won't usually be a problem. Meals, routine care and the times when the baby wants to be picked up, add up to an ample period when there will be good learning opportunities. With older children, mealtimes still provide plenty of opportunities for conversations and play, but it will probably be necessary at times for parents to make a deliberate effort to set aside periods of the day when a child can rely on a one-to-one interaction.

This is not to imply that these periods should be ones that are always filled with deliberate activities, or ones in which parents invariably put a specific emphasis on learning. Even at times when parents are especially keen to encourage learning, it may often turn out that their child is too easily distracted, too tired, or too irritable to cooperate for long, or is simply not interested. On these occasions there is nothing to be gained from being overly persistent. Like older people, children do not want to feel that they are being pushed. Sometimes, 'doing things together' may involve a relatively passive, low-key activity such as watching television together. Yet even then, there is a world of difference between a child simply watching on her own, and sharing that experience with a parent who can be counted upon to answer questions, provide explanations, respond to comments, enjoy jokes and generally help to make the experience more fun.

Interactions that are intellectually challenging can occur at mealtimes, or when parent and child are watching television, or engaged on household tasks, or when they are doing nothing in particular. So although occasions when parents have deliberately set aside times for play activities do present special advantages, there are many other times and events in everyday life that are valuable in providing opportunities to explain things and give encouragement.

THE APPROACH OF THIS BOOK

This book has been designed to serve as a handbook that can be referred to as often as necessary. In most of the chapters there are practical instructions about specific everyday learning activities, lists of things to do, and 'how to' advice of various kinds. Some of the principles underlying early childhood learning may be outlined prior to our suggesting specific activities designed to encourage or develop particular skills, so parents will understand why a particular practical activity is being introduced and how it will contribute to their child's progress. The majority of the games and activities described here are identical to, or based upon, those that have been demonstrated to be effective in research studies investigating learning and development in young children.

It is sometimes necessary to counter the *bad* advice to parents that is all too available. For example, there exist various common fallacies which, for those parents who believe them to be true, can seriously hamper their efforts to encourage a child's progress. Typical examples are, 'Leave teaching to the teachers', 'Don't try to help your child learn X or Y until the child is old enough to be "ready"', 'Avoid baby talk', 'Children will learn to talk by themselves when they decide they want to', and 'Television is bad for children'. Later chapters explain what is wrong – and in some cases potentially harmful – with misleading assertions like these. In these chapters there is less stress on games and activities and more emphasis on ways of encouraging the growing child.

You will have a lot of fun encouraging your child to learn. Anyone who spends a few minutes observing parents with their children in the aisles of a supermarket will not fail to notice that some adults generally enjoy their children's company and others do not. If you are not certain which of these is you, you can be sure that in discovering how to help your children learn more successfully you will also find greater pleasure in sharing your daily activities with them.

In summary

To summarize what parents should aim for:

- Do things together
- Make sure that there are times when your child has all your attention
- Share your everyday activities with your children; include them in as much as possible of your daily life
- Talk *with* your children, not *at* them, and create plenty of opportunities when you and the child can respond to one another
- Enjoy lots of games together
- Never criticize your young child's efforts
- Make a big effort to see life from your child's point of view
- Be serious about guiding your child towards learning and discovery

The following chapters will help you put these intentions into practice.

| First Steps in Learning

Tom is only four weeks old, and at first glance he does not yet seem able to perceive very much. But if you listen carefully to his hungry cries, you may notice that they begin to stop just before he is picked up to be fed. This tells us that Tom, who has noticed his mother's face above him, has already learned from previous experience that food can be expected shortly. If Tom's mother turns and walks away without picking him up she will find the cries get louder again.

This chapter concentrates on how babies in their first year can be encouraged to make progress. Learning soon begins to make a difference in a baby's life. Sophie, who is a few days younger than Tom, has also started to make sense of things. She already acts in ways that tell us she makes use of what she has learned. For instance, she usually continues crying after she has been picked up, but she starts calming down as her mother carries her into the room where she will be fed. Sophie has learned to connect feeding with the experience of being in that room. If her mother were to take her to a different place Sophie would immediately become agitated again.

Sophie and Tom are both demonstrating that what they have learned is already starting to make a contribution to their lives. They have learned to anticipate significant occasions. They are beginning to gain knowledge that makes important aspects of their everyday world predictable, and that is a big step towards bringing some aspects of their lives under control. Even at one month, daily events for both Tom and Sophie are starting to have some kind of order and pattern. For each of them, the world is no longer the series of random happenings that it appeared to be when they were first born.

Within the next two or three months, Sophie and Tom will have gained quite a sophisticated understanding of how different aspects of their lives concur. By then, as research has demonstrated, if you show these babies movie films they will have a clear preference for those films in which speech and lip movements are properly synchronized. This tells us that a definite expectation of speech messages has been formed, based on the baby's experiences. The finding that young babies have formed such a preference proves that they are already able to memorize information. In fact, research has also demonstrated that as early as two months babies can remember visual objects shown to them a week previously.

LEARNING IN NEWBORNS

Babies begin life well equipped to make use of learning opportunities. Newborns can see patterns and they respond to human faces, preferring these to other objects. They can even distinguish between different facial expressions. They can hear at birth, and in the first week of life they can already distinguish their mother's voice. They are soon busy exploring. During the first week they will turn towards objects to bring them into sharper visual focus. Newborns can also move their heads in response to sounds. They will move in the direction of someone who speaks a word, but if the same word is continually repeated the head turning will eventually stop until a new word is uttered. It is as if, for the infant, the novelty has worn off.

Babies waste no time in getting on with the business of learning. Even in the first week babies use their mouths to investigate new objects, and they quickly learn to explore hard and soft objects differently. Before the end of the first month a baby will have connected voices and faces. She will get quite upset if the mother's voice is heard coming from the 'wrong' location – somewhere other than her face.

If a newborn hears the same sound every time she starts receiving milk, she will soon start sucking when the sound occurs on its own. That tells us that the baby has learned to link the two events. In the first week babies can learn to vary their rate of sucking in order to produce the reward of hearing the mother's voice, which they already prefer to that of another person. So if sucking more slowly leads to the mother's voice and sucking faster produces another voice, the infant will suck more slowly. If the consequences of sucking faster or more slowly are then reversed the same baby will speed up the rate of sucking.

Babies are born with a wide range of reflexes, some of which fade and are replaced by learned skills. With these, the baby can choose to respond or not. For example, a newborn baby has a 'grasp' reflex which enables her to grasp an object or finger presented to her. By three or four months the involuntary reflex has been integrated into a grasping movement which is under the baby's control.

By around four months, babies are starting to have some active control over the events that make up their lives. At this age they will show obvious pleasure when they make something happen. They seem to enjoy doing things for their own sake, perhaps because this gives them a feeling of mastery. Moving a toy or knocking it down, or just making a noise, will be enough to delight the baby.

When you are playing with your baby, one way in which you can help her at this stage is to create situations where it is easy for her to make things happen. She will begin to learn that her own actions can affect her surroundings. Modest as these achievements may seem to adult eyes, they are important because they signal the beginnings of the child's long journey towards independence.

ATTENDING AND EXPLORING

At eight months, Rachel is a full-time explorer. Any toy you give her will be submitted to close inspection. After she has examined all its possibilities she will turn her attention to other things, but while she is concentrating on one item she is not easily distracted. Even in her earliest days the way she used her mouth to explore objects gave the impression that she was learning about them, just as she now learns by using her hands. Rachel is less restless and impulsive than many babies and she does not become bored so easily. She gives the impression of deciding what to do before she acts. She has learned that paying careful attention to the objects she encounters is a good way of finding out about all kinds of interesting things.

Some babies are more easily distracted than Rachel, finding it hard to restrain their impulsiveness and avoid switching their attention when there is something new to look at. Babies like these need to be encouraged to attend to things for longer. At all ages, being able to concentrate on the task at hand is a key to successful learning. How can we help those more impulsive babies? One of the best ways for parents to encourage a longer attention span is to help their baby focus on activities or objects which are particularly helpful or informative for her. Later in the chapter we give lots of practical ways of helping babies. People who can give close and undivided attention to something increase the likelihood of remembering it, and this is just as true of infants as it is of adults. Babies who are good at concentrating on things also tend to become skilful and knowledgeable youngsters.

Even during the first months of a baby's life efforts to stimulate learning will make a real difference. That does not mean that all babies who are encouraged to learn during the first six months will inevitably turn into capable adults, or that babies who receive relatively little stimulation at this stage can never catch up. All the same, making good early progress will bring useful advantages.

How can parents and carers encourage a baby during the first six months of life? At this stage there is no point in setting specific goals, and a 'what shall I teach my child today?' approach is not at all appropriate. It is wiser to aim at helping a baby to get into the habit of exploring and attending than to be concerned about particular achievements.

In the following section some play activities are described that meet three realistic goals for the infant learner.

- First, there are activities that provide opportunities and encouragement for a baby to practise giving careful attention to objects and events.
- Second, there are play activities that encourage the baby to explore.
- Third, we describe activities that are designed to help the baby draw upon attending and exploring skills, and begin to experience a degree of mastery or control over parts of her life.

Things to do

Encouraging attention

As we have seen, it is a good idea for parents to aim at what some researchers call 'encouragement of attention' in their young babies. These are some things you can do to help your baby to attend to, and concentrate on, objects, events and pictures.

- Introduce your baby to similarities and differences in the objects she encounters. You might try stroking her hand over something smooth and then over something rough, or over two blankets with different textures. It may seem pointless to say 'rough' or 'smooth' to a child when you know that it will be months before she will be capable of using the word, but it will help her gain the idea that word sounds and qualities go together.
- If your baby is already interested in something, she will be receptive to learning more about it. Take your cue from her. Take time to see what she is looking at. Point to an object she is already concentrating on, and name it or make a comment about it.
- Encourage your baby to make eye contact with you. Raising the pitch of your voice can help to achieve this. 'Making faces' is another way to gain and hold a baby's attention. Many parents do these things instinctively.
- Be prepared for the fact that sometimes your baby will not be at all interested in something you are keen to share with her. That is quite natural: there are many possible reasons. She may be attending to something else, or preoccupied with different needs. Above all, don't feel that you have failed, and remember that she is not deliberately rejecting your efforts. If she is definitely not interested, don't push it. There will be plenty more opportunities later.

Encouraging exploration

For curious humans of all ages, exploring is one of the best ways of finding out important information about our environment. Exploring helps people survive. For a baby it is the way to find the answer to important questions: 'what's out there?' 'how do things work?' 'what leads to what?' 'what events go together?' 'how do I get this object to work?' It is not at all surprising that researchers have found that babies who are allowed to be active explorers in the early months become knowledgeable and skilful children. In one study it was discovered that those babies whose exploring activities were particularly effective and successful tended to be ones whose mothers actively encouraged them in this.

- Don't forget that for a young baby simple physical circumstances have a big influence upon opportunities to explore. For instance, a baby who is being held or carried will be in a much better position to see interesting sights than one lying in a cot. So when you pick up a crying baby to soothe her you are also helping to give her a more interesting environment to look at. Because they enjoy exploring, it is hardly surprising that most babies like to be picked up and held when they are alert.
- As well as drawing your baby's attention to an object, you might show how it can be used. This will help her to learn about what she is looking at. For instance, you might tap on a toy to show how it will move or make a noise. Effectively, you are playing together, and showing that there are lots of different ways to explore.
- Depending on the particular object, activities such as banging, squeezing, shaking, manipulating, investigating with the mouth, may provide fun and information for a baby. Of course, babies will often discover new ways to explore things on their own, but parents can help by suggesting additional possibilities.
- When exploring something with a baby, it can be helpful to guide her hands directly. For instance, with a toy that pulls apart, or a box with a lid, helping the child to do the necessary movements at first will draw

her attention to an interesting activity that she will eventually learn to do for herself.

- Be sensitive to your baby's preferences. She will have her own likes and dislikes. Some babies like loud bangs: others hate them. There is no need to worry if your neighbour's baby loves to listen to a song and yours does not. That doesn't mean that your child will never learn to enjoy music, and there is certainly no harm in encouraging her to listen to sounds. Respect your child's individuality, and don't expect her to share all your own enthusiasms.

- Encourage your baby to explore an item with more than one of her senses. Babies are surprisingly good at recognizing that an object which they have explored with (say) the mouth is the same as one they have inspected visually. A single toy may yield different rewards when it is banged, looked at, or placed in the mouth. If your baby does not catch on to the idea of using a different sense to explore a toy she is looking at, don't be afraid to show her how.

Encouraging mastery and control

People of all ages need to feel in control. Children and adults who don't feel that they have enough control over their own lives may experience frustration and anxiety. Those who are convinced that their own actions will make a difference tend to be confident and happy, and set themselves challenging goals.

The development of a sense of being in control starts in infancy, when a baby learns that some of her actions have reliable and predictable outcomes. Even a newborn whose sucking movements produce milk is already beginning to make things happen. Psychologists have found that babies benefit from being put in a variety of situations where their actions have a reliable outcome.

- When your baby is around three months old, try tying a bell on a ribbon gently round her wrist. She will soon learn to her delight that she can produce a nice sound by her own movements. (Use a bell that has no separate parts, which could be dangerous. Stay with your baby while she is wearing it.)
- Experiment by attaching bells to other parts of the baby's body, such as the ankle, or arrange things so that moving one limb produces one sound and moving another limb produces a different noise. In this way you can help your baby to learn, first, that her actions make things happen and, later, that different actions have different consequences.
- Play a gentle game of tug-of-war with your baby. Give her opportunities to experience the effects of her movements and discover what can be achieved by pushing and pulling.
- Before your baby can sit up on her own, encourage her to participate as much as she can. If you lift her only slowly and with the minimum force she will help to pull herself up and make it clear that she has enjoyed achieving this.
- When your baby can successfully reach for objects, try placing a toy just outside her reach, so that she has to make a special effort to grasp it. It is important to ensure that her efforts are regularly successful. Too much frustration will lead to tears.
- Encourage your baby to make all sorts of different things happen, through what she herself does. Babies like to see bricks tumbling down, and they like wheels that go round and toys that roll along the floor.
- Help your child to learn that things can be controlled

indirectly, even when she cannot touch them. Let her discover that she can pull a toy truck on a string, and that when she cannot reach a toy the string can help her to pull it towards her.

- Let your baby know that you are impressed by her activities, so that she can learn that actions have positive social consequences as well as physical ones. You can do this by clapping and smiling, and also by appreciative sounds and language. Words that express your delight ('That's lovely!' for instance) will be enjoyed by your baby well before she can fully understand them. Your response is part of the baby's reward.

- Older babies, who are now mobile, enjoy games in which they search for objects which you have hidden. As well as helping babies to learn that objects are still there even when they cannot see them, hide and seek games provide another good way to learn that making an effort to do something can have rewarding consequences. Try to make sure that your baby succeeds without too much delay: failure can be discouraging.

A final word

The activities described in this chapter will help your baby to make excellent progress in her first year. But to be really effective in helping your child to learn, you need to become fully attuned to her particular needs and temperament, and discover how to respond in ways that take account of her particular personality. The next chapter looks at ways of doing so.

3 | Being a Responsive Guide

Edward is three months old and he thoroughly enjoys being picked up – not only because he enjoys the closeness and attention from his mother, but because he likes to see what is going on around him. Being held gives him an opportunity to see the world from a safe, comfortable place, and of course he learns a great deal from this experience.

George, also three months old, does not find being picked up quite so enjoyable. His mother has noticed that George can become overwhelmed and made anxious by all he sees when he is held up. The amount of stimulation he gets at these times can be too much for him, because he is unusually sensitive to visual information. So while for Edward the consequence of being picked up by his mother is to give him interesting things to look at, picking him up does not bring quite the same benefits for George.

Of course, providing a baby with extra visual stimulation is by no means the only reason for picking him up; doing so has plenty of other happy consequences. All the same, it is clear that as far as learning about the visual world is concerned, what is true for Edward is not true for George.

George and Edward are both lucky in having mothers who are already well attuned to the particular personalities and temperaments of their babies. Every baby is unique, and even when they are small, children differ from one another as to how they experience, and learn from, the events that make up their lives. Most babies are cuddly, but there are some who do not like to be held or cuddled. Some babies are usually calm when awake, others are prone to be irritable. Some babies, as we saw in the previous chapter, are attentive from the beginning, while others are impulsive and easily distracted. When distressed, some babies are easily soothed but others are not. Babies also differ considerably in their activity levels and in the time they spend sleeping. All these variables have an effect on how different babies learn, and on their aptitudes and interests.

This chapter, like the previous one, concentrates on babies who have not yet learned to talk, but it introduces a number of principles and suggestions that also apply to toddlers and older children. Parents who provide positive learning environments for their children do not achieve this just by keeping to a list of 'correct' teaching activities. It is equally important to discover what games and experiences are appropriate for a particular child, and when, something which is possible only when parents are aware of their child's individual needs and preferences. So while you do not need formal teaching skills in order to encourage young children to learn, it is important to make an effort to 'tune in' to the temperament and moods of an individual child. Some parents find this easier than others, but there is nothing mysterious about it: it is largely a matter of getting into the habit of giving your baby undivided attention for a while, consciously putting aside other concerns.

GETTING ATTUNED TO YOUR BABY'S STATE

On the whole, babies only learn when they are in the right frame of mind. They are not attentive when tired, or irritable, fractious, or hungry, and they do not learn well when they are anxious, afraid, or over-excited. The best times for learning activities are those occasions when a baby is quiet and calm but alert.

It takes time for new parents to recognize when their baby is in a state of quiet alertness and to make the best use of this time. Knowing when becomes easier as you get more familiar with the way she expresses different moods. Take care to avoid making the baby too excited or over-aroused if you want to encourage a calm, alert mood.

Mary Ainsworth, a psychologist who has spent much of her career observing mothers and children together, found ample evidence that children really do benefit from parents who put an effort into being attuned and responsive to their needs. She observed that such parents tend to have happier babies who make better progress than those whose parents are not so sensitive to their needs. Other researchers have discovered that children whose parents were responsive to their facial expressions, vocalizations and body movements in the first six months tended to score highly at intelligence tests administered when they were four years old.

You can't always be a perfect parent, of course, nor is it desirable for a child to have constant parental attention, one hundred per cent of the time. If you get into the habit of regularly giving your child individual attention, however, it is easier to take time for yourself without feeling guilty. And a baby who has been given well-focused attention for substantial periods will learn to practise new skills independently.

Becoming 'sensitive' to or 'attuned' to the needs of babies and young children is partly a matter of being able to understand the child's point of view – something we touched on in Chapter 1. Almost all parents make an effort to be sensitive to their babies' needs, but for most of us there are times when our own feelings get in the way. On difficult days when it seems that a child is never going to stop crying we may start to think that she is crying just to annoy or dominate us. When we are particularly upset we may begin to believe that a toddler is making unreasonable efforts to get attention, although when we are calmer and more rational we know perfectly well that a young child's hunger for attention is just as genuine as any other need. The need for attention can seem to vary from day to day: sometimes a child appears much more demanding than usual, especially if we are feeling below par.

If we get locked into negative ways of reacting we run the risk of being less than sensitive to the real needs of our children, because we are looking at what happens only from our own point of view. On reflection, the very idea of a six month old baby deliberately setting out to manipulate her parents seems pretty silly. But Mary Ainsworth has noted that some parents do habitually regard their child's actions in these negative terms. Such parents may be no less loving or caring than others, but are too preoccupied with their own desires and emotions to be fully aware of their child's individual needs, and her particular ways of expressing those needs.

Ainsworth observed that in some cases worried or unhappy parents' thoughts are frequently geared to their own wishes, moods and activities, so that their perceptions are dominated by their own concerns. This, naturally, affects the way in which they act towards their children, as the parent is largely unaware of the various signals by which a child communicates his needs, fears, and anxieties. Such a parent will not be very responsive to the particular needs of the child.

Most of us have experienced times when the demands of parenthood seem overwhelming, making it difficult to be sensitive to children's needs. When we are hurried we may wrongly interpret any slowing in a baby's rate of feeding as a sign that he is becoming full. A preoccupied parent may misinterpret her baby's behaviour as a sign that she is tired, and put her back to bed when the baby is actually wanting to be picked up and cuddled. A parent may mistakenly perceive her baby's fractious behaviour as a sign that she is rejecting the parent's attentions.

In contrast, Mary Ainsworth notes that when parents are attuned to the different signals (including various kinds of vocalizations, body movements and facial expressions), by which a baby sends out information about herself, they can pick up subtle communications and interpret even the smallest cues. They may not always interpret the baby's signals correctly, but they learn from their own mistakes. So their responses to their child are usually appropriate as well as prompt. This doesn't mean being over-indulgent or always giving a baby what she demands, but it is important to acknowledge the message conveyed by the baby, and try to make some sort of appropriate response.

The process of responsive parenting is two-way: you learn from the baby and the baby learns from you. It takes time and experience to 'read' accurately your baby's emotional, practical and developmental needs, especially before a child is able to tell you. No one can be totally responsive at all times, and there is no reason to feel guilty because we cannot always be highly sensitive to our children's every need or exquisitely attuned to their signals. Take heart: if you regularly give your child your full attention, you will already be half way there.

Things to do

Improving your ability to 'read' your child

This section contains some broad practical guidelines for parents who feel they want to increase their sensitivity and responsiveness to their babies. More specific suggestions are provided in other chapters, in particular those that highlight language and communication.

Mary Ainsworth lists four components of parental sensitivity that are especially important in the first year of a baby's life. These are:

> **1 Being aware of the signals and messages by which a baby communicates information about herself**
>
> **2 Accurately interpreting the baby's signals**
>
> **3 Making an appropriate response**
>
> **4 Making a prompt response**

Doing all these is not always easy. With 1 and 4 the most essential thing is to make sure that your baby really is getting your full attention, for without it you will not be aware of all the messages the baby is sending you. You certainly won't be able to respond to them promptly.

Points 2 and 3 are less straightforward. Much depends on a parent's willingness to learn by trial and error, to work patiently on ways of communicating with the baby.

Quiet alertness

Earlier in this chapter we talked about 'quiet alertness', that state of mind when a baby is most able to attend to objects and events in the outside world. As you become more attuned to your baby, you will begin to recognize these times.

In the first week of life, a baby is likely to be in a quiet and alert state for periods of about ten minutes, usually after feeding or a bowel movement. These are the best times for activities which encourage a young baby to learn. By the end of the first month, about one-fifth of the baby's waking life is spent in a state of quiet alertness, and the length of time goes on increasing as the child gets older.

You may be able to extend your baby's mood of quiet

alertness. Good ways to achieve this include the following:

- Hold the baby in an upright position or, if this brings your faces too close together, seat her securely in a baby-seat and sit facing her, about eight to ten inches away.
- Vary the way in which you talk to her; alter the pitch of your voice, for instance.
- Establish eye contact and help to hold it by using animated and varied facial expressions; for example, opening the eyes widely and raising the eyebrows, opening the mouth, giving a large smile.
- If she becomes fractious, sing gently to her or play soothing music.
- Gently rock the baby. As well as having a soothing effect which helps to stop them becoming too highly aroused, rocking helps babies to follow and focus on moving objects. Researchers have discovered that look-ing at things when in motion provides opportunities for a baby's perceptual development. Keep rocking movements smooth, gentle and slow. Avoid jigging, which will arouse rather than soothe.
- Some experts believe that 'swaddling' a baby by firmly wrapping a blanket around the arms and legs will help to promote a state of quiet alertness. Babies seem to enjoy the warmth and security, and it is also possible that swaddling helps prevent them from being startled by their own reflex movements. Some research evidence suggests that when recently fed babies are swaddled they cry less, sleep better, and are calmer.
- Imitate your baby's own facial expressions – responding in this way both engages your baby's interest and encourages interactions between you. As the baby grows older you can start to take it in turns to be active and attentive.

- Avoid overwhelming your baby with too much stimulation. Give her time to 'reply' to your responses.

4 | Getting Ready for Language

A great many parents instinctively talk to their babies, although language development is rarely at the forefront of your mind when your child is less than a year old. That communication is vital: for although children don't begin to talk until around the end of the first year, active speech is the product of a great deal of language learning, certainly not its beginning.

Babies whose parents regularly talk to them from an early age learn essential communication skills that language depends upon. They gradually learn how to make the sounds that language uses, and discover that sounds can represent objects and experiences. They learn that these sounds play a part in communicating with other people. And well before they start talking, babies begin to learn the art of holding conversations, each partner taking turns to communicate with the other.

These 'pre-language' communicative abilities are important in their own right, and they also provide the foundation that spoken language is built upon. Parents who deliberately make conversation with their babies are, in fact, doing an enormously important job. Speech is only possible when a child has progressed through various pre-language phases, where a good deal of preparatory work is done.

ENCOURAGING EARLY PROGRESS

Some experts used to believe that there was little point in making special efforts to encourage early language development, because there was only scanty evidence that such efforts made a real difference. However, the findings of recent investigations show that parents' efforts to encourage their child's language development can have extremely positive effects. Psychologist Gordon Wells, who recorded parents and children in their homes recognized that the sheer amount of talk by parents and the length of their utterances was not crucial, but he found that the children who made the most rapid language development were those whose parents were more responsive than others to their child's attempts to communicate. These children's parents were more likely to acknowledge what they said, imitate them or repeat statements, ask their child questions, and talk about the child's activities.

In other words, the children who made the best progress were those whose parents attended closely to the children's attempts to communicate their needs and interests. By talking about topics that concerned the child, these parents made sure that there were good opportunities for language development to take place. They also tended to give their child more instructions, which was especially helpful when these were related to activities in which the child was already engaged. A child finds it easier to make sense of words which are directly linked to something she is already thinking about. Questions about an activity that the child is already involved in are similarly useful, especially if the questions are open-ended. And, following on from Gordon Wells' research, there is now further evidence that children do make especially good progress when they hear speech that refers to objects, events and experiences that are already engaging their attention.

Children benefit very considerably when parents consistently use everyday opportunities to help them to increase their language and communication skills. To help make that possible, practical language activities make up much of the remainder of this chapter. However, for language activities and games to be effective they need to be broadly in phase with the child's current stage of development. At this stage it is helpful to have a brief overview of the steps babies and young children go through on the way towards mastering their native language.

LAYING THE FOUNDATIONS OF EARLY LANGUAGE

At birth, babies already have some of the hearing skills they will need in order to interpret speech. Even in the first month they show a preference for human sounds and can recognize their mother's voice. The communication skills of newborns are limited of course, but a variety of 'signalling' functions are achieved by crying, sucking, facial expressions, noises and body movements. These enable the infant to make contact with the adult carer. Most of the baby's first sounds are involuntary, yet even the earliest cries and gurgles help the infant to learn to move the vocal organs and control the flow of air through the mouth and nose.

By the end of the second month most babies make 'cooing' sounds that are distinct from crying noises. Cooing often contains sounds that are similar to consonants and vowels, and cooing responses may be strung together in series. Cooing assists the baby's growing mastery of sounds, helping her learn to control and coordinate the movements of numerous muscles in the vocal organs with those of the tongue.

By the fourth month many babies will be producing

recognizable chuckles, and may also have started to imitate the lip movements of their carers. By this time the baby's ability to perceive speech sounds has also progressed. As early as the fourth week some infants can tell some consonants and vowels apart.

Early signs that a baby is beginning to *understand* language can also be present by the fourth month, when babies can now distinguish between different tones of voice. By now many parents and babies will have got into the habit of having 'conversations', where they respond to each other in turn. At first, these conversations will be somewhat one-sided, with the mother responding in words or other sounds to the baby's cries or gurgles. Sooner or later, however, these sessions become real dialogues, parent and baby responding to each other's utterances with obvious enjoyment.

Real comprehension may start between months six and nine: at this age some phrases are clearly understood, as is apparent when an often repeated phrase like 'Where's Daddy?' makes a baby turn towards the door.

As babies approach six months they produce clearer, more controlled sounds, which are often repeated many times. The actual sounds that appear at this stage may involve changes in pitch, or trills or bubbly noises. As with cooing, this sound play provides valuable practice, and soon leads to the familiar consonant-vowel sequences (dadada, for instance) which are called 'babbling'.

Babbling has no clear meaning, although the actual sounds uttered are often similar to words. But about the time when babbling becomes established, babies do start to communicate meaningfully in other ways. They often point at things, and look at objects that another person points at.

By around nine months a greater variety of sounds is appearing. Utterances are now beginning to have some of the rhythmic qualities and fluency we associate with 'real' language. Around this age babies listen very closely, and the sounds they make begin to reflect the particular language spoken by their parents. This is why the speech of deaf children starts to sound distinctly abnormal: although they may have cooed and babbled like hearing babies, they now cannot properly hear the sounds which other babies are beginning to imitate successfully.

Around the end of a baby's first year, we start to hear the repeated use of sounds which, because they are clear and appear to have a definite meaning, parents are happy to call their child's first words. At this time the child's ability to understand words will be well ahead of her capacity to speak. By now she may already comprehend ten or twenty different words, although she cannot say them all.

Things to do

In this section we describe a number of games and activities which encourage language development. The word 'encourage' is used deliberately. The best and most effective help a parent can offer generally takes the form of creating opportunities, encouraging a child's attempts, responding enthusiastically, questioning, making requests, sharing experiences with a child and inviting some participation in your activities. Very little actual 'instruction' is involved.

Don't expect progress to be regular and straightforward: it is much more likely to be uneven and unpredictable, and remember that every baby is unique. The activity that the baby next door just loves may leave yours cold.

If your child does not enjoy the game you have chosen, back off and try something else. You can always introduce it again later. Sometimes a child will not be interested in playing any of the games you offer. If that happens, it is probably because she is not currently in a state of quiet alertness. Perhaps she is tired, irritable, over-aroused or hungry. If necessary, refer to the list of suggested ways to achieve and maintain a state of quiet alertness that is at the end of Chapter 3.

Activities for the first six months

Conversations form a vital part of human communication. Babies can start to learn about them in the first six months.

- Start by giving the baby your full attention, and keep her in face-to-face contact, about eight to ten inches away.
- Try to make sure the baby is attending to you. She needs to be doing so before you can properly begin any conversation. Raising the pitch of your voice will help hold your baby's attention.
- At first you can simply respond to your baby's sounds, perhaps by commenting and smiling ('That's a lovely squelch') or imitating her noises, or making a new sound of your own. Then give your baby time to make a response.
- In early dialogues it is a good idea for the parent to imitate any sounds the infant makes. If your child coos, try cooing back. Doing so will help to initiate sequences of taking turns.
- If your baby is feeling quiet you can imitate her facial expression. Although a dialogue based mainly on visual responses might not seem to be the real thing, it does incorporate some of the most important elements of a conversation, such as communicating, attending to the other person, and taking turns.
- Don't be afraid to try communicating new sounds or new facial expressions, but always keep to activities that you both enjoy. As with other games and activities,

don't try to continue when your child ceases to enjoy it.
- In the first few months, don't be disappointed if your baby's responses are not vocal. All the same, try to establish a routine in which you and she each take turns: one saying (or doing) something while the other attends to it. Alternate who is the active one, and who is attentive.

Remember, give your baby time to respond. Don't rush her!

Games and activities for months five to eight

There are adults who find it natural and easy to talk to babies, but not everyone does. If it is something you find difficult, give yourself time to get used to the idea and to overcome any self-consciousness or embarrassment.

There is no harm in baby talk. You do not have to worry about the possibility of your child learning 'wrong' language in the first year. At this age the main aim is learning to communicate. Baby talk can help a parent and baby to enjoy communicating, perhaps because it provides greater simplicity or exaggeration, or more repetition (choo-choo, gee-gee) than adult talk. It is important that you communicate in a way in which you feel comfortable, and this may or may not include baby talk.

It is useful to regard yourself as 'feeding' the baby with language; get into the habit of doing this from the earliest months. There are many ways to go about it, but it takes more than just exposing the child to words. What is particularly important is that your language be directed towards your baby and her own interests. Here are a few general guidelines:

- Talk *to* the baby, not *at* her, and if you can talk about an object or toy in which she is currently showing interest, so much the better.

- Always try to give a baby time to make some kind of response to what you say. Do not talk without allowing opportunities for her to respond.
- When you are talking to your baby, give her your full attention, and try to establish and maintain eye contact.
- Talk about things that are already familiar to a baby, such as parts of the child's body, a familiar toy, household objects, bathtime or feeding activities. Keep to the here and now. Use verbs that denote actions as well as nouns that label things. Get into the habit of telling a child the names of common objects and actions well before you think she is capable of understanding words. Research has shown that the more parents provide the words for things, the larger their babies' vocabularies.
- Make it easy for your baby to pay attention to you by reducing distractions; turn off any background noise.
- If you are not sure what to talk about it is a good idea to hold a kind of running commentary in which you talk to your baby about what is happening and what you are doing. Repeat words and phrases to help them become familiar.
- Pitch your voice slightly high, something many do quite naturally when talking to babies. Most babies are especially sensitive to high-pitched sounds, and they may not hear the low-pitched sounds we make when having an adult conversation. A lot of people, self-conscious men in particular, find it embarrassing to speak in a higher pitch; if this is difficult for you, try talking in a falsetto voice when you and your baby are alone in the privacy of your own home. You may be gratified by your baby's reaction.
- Sing to your baby. This is a good way to calm an anxious baby or soothe one who is over-aroused. It also encourages babies to attend to sounds.

- Songs accompanied by appropriate activities ('Rock-a-bye Baby', for example) help babies begin to understand that sounds and activities can be connected.

Activities and games to introduce from around month nine

- Frequently accompany language with actions. Rhymes and songs that involve doing this – 'Pat-a-cake', 'This little piggy went to market' for instance – are helpful. It is also a good idea to accompany everyday playful activities with language: 'Here comes my finger'; 'I'm going to kiss your nose'; 'Up we go'.
- Many children will want to take a more active role in games like 'Pat-a-cake', and they will imitate your own actions. Encourage this, and also encourage your baby to imitate other gestures that go with words, such as a wave for 'goodbye' or a gesture of greeting for 'hello'.
- Don't be reticent about endlessly repeating words and providing lots of opportunities for them to become familiar to your baby. If you draw attention to an object, you can keep naming it while you are talking about it. For example, 'Here's teddy. What a nice teddy. Teddy's coming to see you. Can you stroke teddy?'
- Keep things simple and concrete. Use simple sentences, such as 'I touch the ball.' 'You touch the ball.'
- For obvious reasons it is always sensible to talk slowly and clearly when addressing a baby. You should also make an effort to incorporate considerably more variation in your speech than usual. As well as varying pitch and intonation you can exaggerate words or phrases. Try accompanying them with distinctive facial expressions.
- Introduce picture books to your baby as early as you

like. Books provide useful and enjoyable talking points. (Chapter 7 has plenty of suggestions about particular books to choose.) It is sensible to encourage a baby to become familiar with books, learn how to handle them and turn the pages, and discover how to recognize objects when they are depicted in pictures.

- Games of 'Can you say . . . ?' provide lots of good language opportunities for babies from around six months of age. It is often a good idea to start with a word based on sounds that the child has just been babbling. You will have to be prepared for the baby to ignore many of these questions, especially at first. Some babies seem to get more enjoyment than others from imitating sounds.

- Towards the end of the first year, as babies begin to understand the meanings of words, most parents like to test their baby's knowledge by asking questions: 'Which is the teddy?' for example, or 'where is your spoon?' When you do this, do be patient and give your child plenty of time to respond. A baby may be able to understand a word but not yet able to demonstrate that knowledge by pointing. And don't overdo the questioning if your child doesn't seem to be in the mood. Like anyone else, babies don't like to feel that they are always being tested.

5 | Language In Years Two and Three

There are great variations in the age at which children say their first words. Take Jeff, for example, now eighteen months old. He hardly spoke at all until three months ago, but four weeks later he could say ten different words. The number has now increased to around forty. His understanding of words is way ahead of that; at his first birthday he could understand at least twelve words. Now the figure is well over a hundred.

Some of the brightest people are late talkers, of whom Einstein is one example. They say little or nothing other than babble-talk until they reach eighteen months or even older. There is no need to worry if your son or daughter still does not talk much at around twenty months. But if an eighteen month old does not say any words at all and does not even seem to understand language it would be a good idea to have her hearing checked. Hearing problems can hold back language development and are best discovered as soon as possible, well before the child reaches three years.

During the second year, children typically understand about five times as many words as they can speak. It is difficult to be precise because understanding is not an all-or-nothing process. It takes time for a child to understand the range of meanings that a particular word has for an adult.

Most children pass through a stage in which 'Daddy' seems to mean any man and all animals are called 'dog'. If you find that surprising, try putting yourself in the child's position. Imagine you see a four-legged creature with a rider crossing a field, and the adult standing beside you points to them and says 'cheval'. You try to figure out what 'cheval' refers to. Is it the rider, or the animal, or both? Does the word just mean the particular person and/or animal you were looking at or others like them as well? Or was the adult describing something else entirely, the movement of the horse and rider perhaps, the sound of galloping, or something completely different? Just to confuse things even more, the same horse and rider appear again five minutes later, and this time your adult companion shouts out 'Pierre' instead. It is all very puzzling.

In the circumstances, it is entirely natural that children will make mistakes as they try to work out what particular words mean. As well as the kinds of errors that involve giving a word a wider range of meanings that it actually has (for two year old Sally, the word 'moon' refers to almost any round object and 'horsey' seems to mean just about anything that moves fast), a child may also invest a particular word with a much narrower meaning than it in fact possesses. For Tom, 'car' is only his yellow toy racing-car. He will say 'shoe' to refer to his rubber boots but not to his brown lace-ups. And some words will be given a meaning which, as far as adults are concerned, is clearly wrong. Sarah, whose mother pointed out the door to her when someone was coming into the room, now thinks that the word 'door' means anything that opens up.

In a month's time, most of these 'errors' will have gone, but others will have appeared. Understanding the meanings of words can be a somewhat fragile process at first. Yesterday, Robert had no difficulty in pointing to the right toy when his mother said 'Where's the bunny?', but today he just looks blank. There are a number of possible reasons why this may happen, but absolutely no cause for a parent to worry if it does. Often you still won't be sure exactly what it is that your child is trying to express. Does the sentence 'daddy ball' mean that the ball is Daddy's, or that the child has seen Daddy with the ball, or what?

The fact that a child's comprehension runs ahead of her ability to say words can lead to some odd situations. Child psychologist Allysa McCabe relates an anecdote in which a small boy points to his dog and talks to his uncle:

Jim	**Lathy**
Uncle	*Lathy?*
Jim	**No. Lathy**
Uncle	*Oh, you mean Lassie.*
Jim	**Yeth. Lathy**

Before children start to join words together, they sometimes use a single word to perform the task of a whole sentence. When Isabel says 'Dada' it is not always easy to know what she is trying to say. On some occasions the word appears to mean 'I want Daddy', but at other times she seems to be saying 'Let's tell Daddy' or even 'That's my Daddy'.

PUTTING WORDS TOGETHER

At some point, perhaps six months after the first word appears, a child will start to string two words together, which we identify as the beginnings of a sense of grammar. By grammar we do not mean the grammar of adult English. We simply mean that the child has already incorporated some basic rules that govern the order of words. This is apparent from the fact that the child will order words in some ways but not in others. For example, Victoria, twenty-one month old daughter of a child language specialist, made sentences using word combinations such as, 'toy gone', 'that car', 'kiss doll', 'milk gone', 'Daddy there', 'teddy there', 'she cold': but she would never say 'cold that' or 'there kiss'. She did not order her words just randomly.

When a child starts to join words together it is particularly important for parents not to be too concerned about correcting errors. Of course, you will naturally find yourself wanting to guide your child towards language that expresses her intended meaning as clearly as possible. How should you do this? Here is an example of how *not* to help a child communicate better.

Child	**Me got ball.**
Adult	*No, Tom, that's not right. Say 'I've got a ball'.*

Criticism of this sort is likely to confuse Tom; it may also make him anxious and harm his self-esteem. Also, since it will be some time before he has the grammatical skills to produce 'I've got a ball' for himself, there is little point in an adult trying to get him to imitate that sentence. That is not the way language learning works. Here is a better alternative:

Child	**Me got dolly.**
Adult	*Yes, you have, haven't you. And look at me, I've got a dolly and I've got a ball.*

Notice that this adult is communicating in a friendly way that is responsive to what the child is saying. So, for the child, her words are producing a rewarding outcome that encourages her efforts to communicate. At the same time, by expanding on what the child says, the adult is providing an example which will gradually encourage the child to learn a better way of expressing the message.

It is important to remember that language is a way of communicating with people, and not just something to be learned for its own sake. It is worth repeating that there is no need to worry at all about the grammatical correctness of your baby's language, which will take care of itself later.

The important thing is to help your child extend her powers of communication. She is still continuing to learn about having conversations, finding out how to interact with other people in ways that involve give and take by both partners. She needs to explore enjoyable ways of sharing meanings through the language messages she gives and receives.

The child's efforts to communicate will still be relatively crude and inexact, yet there may well be other clues you can use to help interpret what is being expressed. As long as you are giving the child your full attention you may be able to 'read' her facial expression and body movements, and see where her attention is being directed. So the child's language does not have to bear the sole weight of communicating what she is trying to say.

And, paradoxically as it seems at first, when your child begins putting together increasingly long sequences of words, many of the grammatical errors she makes provide excellent demonstrations of the progress she is making. Jane, for instance, who is well into her third year, says:

'I can see mans'
'Mummy comed to see me'
'We seed the doggy'

In these examples, Jane demonstrates an understanding of plurals and past tenses. She is intelligently applying a grammatical rule that she has recently learned, but does not yet know about exceptions to the rules. Her mistakes are similar to errors you would make yourself if you were learning French and didn't yet know all the grammatical rules about irregular verbs.

EXPANDING THE CHILD'S SPEECH

At any time in the second year it can be helpful to start introducing a little more structure into your exchanges with a child. Look at the following dialogue:

Child	Sit chair.
Adult	*Shall I sit in the chair? Do you want me to sit in the chair? OK, I'll sit in the chair [sits in chair].*

Here the adult is starting with the child's intended meaning, and expanding her words into a fuller message which expresses that meaning. She then repeats a more complete way of communicating the message 'sit in the chair', a number of times, and in this way encourages the child to learn fuller patterns of speech.

Quite often, your baby's early efforts will be incomplete as messages as well as grammatically 'incorrect'. In these cases, the adult helps by expanding on the child's words, and perhaps clarifying them as well. A child may not progress immediately to a stage where she says 'sit in the chair' herself. It may be some time before she gains the habit of regularly using an expanded version: '_____ in the _____ ' whenever it is suitable – for example, 'sit in the car', 'walk in the garden'. Yet by repeatedly hearing a parent's expansions a child will gradually come to understand the link between the meaning she is aiming to express and the words in the fuller version which the parent has offered. Eventually the child will learn to incorporate the expanded version in her own sentences, saying for herself 'man on a horse' instead of 'man horse' and 'teddy in the car' instead of 'teddy car'. But you will need to be patient. Even if you regularly expand on your child's brief utterances, it may be some time before she begins to say the extra words herself.

Holding a conversation in which they expand a child's sentences is a way in which parents support their child's early language development. They are providing what some experts call 'language scaffolding', temporary props and supports that form useful aids for the child whose language skills are progressing. A similarly supportive activity is to ask a child questions about what she has just said. This will help draw out her thoughts and give her practice in expressing them in words.

Here are two examples of actual conversations. The first one, where the child was nineteen months old, was recorded by child language specialist Harvey S. Wiener. Notice that the mother's responses all take the form of short questions.

Rachel	**Fly. Big fly!**
Mother	*Where's that fly?*
Rachel	**On door**
Mother	*The fly is on the door?*
Rachel	**Fly on door. Over there!**
Mother	*What should Mummy do?*
Rachel	**Mummy open door.**
Mother	*What happened to the fly?*
Rachel	**Fly flew away. All gone fly.**

The second example is extracted from a conversation recorded by linguist David Crystal. In this case all of the parent's responses take the form of expansions, which are also questions that encourage her child to think and keep the conversation moving.

Child	**Daddy knee**
Mother	*What's that, darling? What about Daddy's knee?*
Child	**Fall-down Daddy.**
Mother	*Did he? Where did he fall down?*
Child	**In-garden fall-down.**
Mother	*Daddy's fallen down in the garden? Poor Daddy. Is he all right?*
Child	**Daddy-knee sore.**

Despite the fact that in years two and three the child's language is moving ahead fast, it needs to be stressed that the activities which best encourage language development are not so very different from those that work well in the first year. There is still no need for any 'instructional' sessions that are not based on games or conversations, or the natural events of everyday life. Just like younger babies, toddlers make good progress with language if their mothers and fathers give them some undivided attention every day and frequently talk to them about objects and events that relate to their current interests and needs. Broadly speaking, the more parent-child conversations the better. Aim to give your child plenty of opportunities to use language and understand it, and plenty of positive feedback and encouragement as well.

Remind yourself from time to time that the best way to help your child is to act as a guide whose job is to do whatever you can to assist her attempts to make sense of the world. You can do this by pointing things out and drawing the child's attention to what is going on, by explaining and helping to make events understandable. Make an effort to anticipate what will interest her and what will confuse her.

Things to do

Language games and activities for one and two year olds

- 'Where is the . . . ?' games have a number of uses, providing opportunities to practise communicating and also encouraging concentration. You can ask questions about parts of the body, toys, household objects, and so on. 'Where is . . . ?' questions about objects pictured in books are especially helpful, and more difficult questions, for example, 'Can you see a white butterfly?', will give opportunities for the child to attend to details. If the child is old enough, encourage her to switch roles with you, so that she asks the questions. Don't be too serious: an occasional deliberate mistake on your part will add enormously to your child's enjoyment.

- 'What's that?' games provide similar opportunities for the child to practise naming and identifying objects, and can lead to other questions and conversations; for example, 'What's the lady doing? . . . and why did she do that?'.

- Labelling and naming activities are still just as helpful as they were in the first year. As well as simply naming objects you can draw attention to all kinds of features and attributes such as colour, shape, size. You can also demonstrate opposites such as biggest, smallest, longest, shortest.

- Whispering is great fun for children, both when you do it and when they try whispering themselves. It is a good way to encourage them to pay careful attention to language sounds.

- Games in which parent and child say and imitate actions, such as 'Wheels go . . .' (round and round), 'Clocks go . . .' (tick-tock) are good because they encourage a child to progress from one-word utterances to sentences. They can be accompanied with movements to depict the actions or by facial expressions – 'Cats go . . .'.

- 'Do what I say' games provide plenty of opportunities for a child to concentrate on language and also to practise connecting words and the movements they represent. You can easily incorporate such games into daily activities, for example, 'Let's walk; now let's stop'. Simple versions of these games will be suitable for children who are just beginning to talk. At this stage they will enjoy following instructions such as 'Touch your ear. Now touch your toe.' Start with one direction at a time – later the child will be able to manage two or even three. When she is old enough, your child will enjoy changing roles, so that she gives the instructions and you follow them. As in 'Where is . . . ?' games, your occasional deliberate errors will be appreciated.

- Demonstrate the meanings of adverbs and prepositions, such as slowly, quickly, under and over, above and below. Use direct actions to demonstrate meanings when possible. Give your child plenty of different examples, or she may fail to generalize. Don't assume that a child who learns the difference between a car going fast and the same car going slowly will automatically know that other objects can move fast or slow: she may assume that the words refer *only* to cars. Act out these concepts yourself and encourage your child to do so.

- When you play 'Do this . . . do that' games in which your child follows your instructions, include ones that involve understanding the prepositions you have introduced. For example, 'Put teddy *under* the table; put the cup *on* teddy's head'. With adverbs, similarly, encourage your child to incorporate their meanings in her actions. For instance, 'Say "hello" quietly, now say "hello" loudly'.

- Get into the habit of regularly encouraging your child to describe and report things that have happened. These might be events that took place recently or ones in a story that you have been reading together. This is a good way of giving a child opportunities to practise expressing her thoughts. It will also provide practice in retrieving items from memory and finding words to describe them. Keep to things that are simple and familiar, and be willing to help by expanding the child's words. Make it clear to her that you are enjoying her efforts to communicate.

- We have already mentioned that young children delight in correcting a parent's deliberate errors. Apart from the fun this creates, it can be a good way to engage a child's attention. If you say 'That's a doggy' and your young son or daughter correctly points out that it is not a dog but a horse, there will be a good opportunity to discuss how people can tell them apart. Children do not learn all the attributes of an object at the same time, so by encouraging a child to look at the similarities and differences between various things you can help her to recognize what contributes to an adult's definition of, say, a horse.

Having conversations with two and three year olds

Listed below are some general principles for developing conversations with toddlers, and some examples of how you can put them into practice. Keep in mind the idea of 'scaffolding', supporting the child's language by providing temporary props for it.

1 Never correct errors in a way that might give a child the impression that her attempts to communicate are 'wrong'.

2 When possible, talk about things that are already engaging the child's interest.

3 To get a conversation started, it is often helpful to ask questions which you think will interest the child.

4 Always give a child plenty of time to respond.

5 If the child does not answer a question, try asking it again, perhaps more simply.

6 Try to be aware of nonverbal communications (facial expressions and bodily movements, for instance) as well as what the child actually says. Quite often these will clarify meanings that would otherwise be ambiguous.

7 Respond (sometimes, but not always) to the child's statements in ways that clarify their meaning. This will usually involve expanding the child's words, and your response will often take the form of a more grammatical version of what (you think) the child seems to be saying. Of course, your interpretation of the child's intended message will not always correspond with what the child aimed to say (as sometimes happens in a conversation between adults) but when this happens the child will probably let you know. Look back at the two examples on page 55.

8 It is often a good idea to make your response to the child's statement in the form of a question, perhaps one that asks for more clarification. Often, your question can incorporate an expansion of the child's words into grammatical language. For example:

Child	**Want do pinano**
Parent	*Why do you want to play the piano?*

More advanced language activities

Some children will find these activities difficult until they are well past their third birthday.

- With three year olds, quite elaborate 'Do what I say' instructions can be introduced. For instance, a 'find the ball' game or one of 'going to the shop' might involve walking to the sofa, turning right, and looking under the table. The occasional bizarre or ridiculous instruction goes down well. All this encourages your child to concentrate on what might come next.

- Talking on the telephone (either a toy telephone or a real one) can help a child learn more about taking turns in conversation. Some children enjoy imitating another person's voice. The first conversations will not go much further than 'hello' and 'goodbye', but you can encourage the child to describe activities: 'Tell Grandma about the boat you went in'. At first, you may need to tell the child what to say: 'Say, "I saw a balloon in the sky"'.

- For some three year olds it will not be too early to encourage them to make up imaginative stories. At first the child will need a large amount of support, with most of the story being provided by you. You can help by providing a beginning that has a broadly familiar structure to those in her story books: 'Once upon a time a little girl called Jennie saw a baby elephant on the other side of road', for example. Then you can say, 'What did she do?'. Don't hurry the child, and if she cannot think of anything you can suggest something to her. You can add some more to the story yourself, after a few sentences encouraging her to make another contribution and tell you how the little girl responded to the next twist in the tale. With practice, your child will be able to take an increasing degree of control for herself.

- Encourage your child to play rhyming games. The importance of rhyming is stressed again in Chapter 8, because rhyming activities give valuable practice at listening carefully to the actual sounds of words. (Research has shown that failure to distinguish between the precise sounds that make up words is a major cause of difficulties in learning how to read.) Make up rhymes whenever you have the opportunity, the more humorous the better. If you find this difficult at first, look out for picture books that introduce rhymes.

6 | Reading to Your Child

Reading aloud to your child may already be a familiar and enjoyable part of your daily routine – or it may be something you are rather hesitant about, uncertain which books are most suitable for the very young. Chapter 7 has lots of ideas here.

This chapter suggests a number of ways in which you and your child can make the best use of time spent reading together. A theme that runs through the chapter is that reading sessions are much more valuable when a child is encouraged to be more than a passive listener. Reading aloud is most beneficial when the child takes an active role, asking questions, commenting on the actions, answering questions posed by the adult, talking about the events and characters in the story and getting into conversations about them. It also needs to be clear from the start that the child's *enjoyment* of reading is absolutely crucial. The best short answer to the question 'How should I read to my child?' is 'In the way that gives the child the greatest fun'.

At the risk of stating the obvious, it is good advice to put as much expression as you can into your reading aloud, and use distinctive voices for different characters. Dramatize as much as you like. Place emphasis on new words that you think your child will like. Enjoy yourself. If you are obviously having fun the chances are that your child will be equally delighted; enjoyment is contagious.

Children's attitudes to being read to vary with their

moods. Sometimes your son or daughter will simply want to listen and won't be interested in talking about the characters, urging you to 'get on with the story'. Sometimes, when you are keen to show your daughter a new book which you are convinced will both delight and stimulate her, she will insist that what she wants is for you to read to her, for the fiftieth time, a familiar story that is threatening to drive you mad with boredom. On these occasions, go along with your child's wishes. Yes, it is true that children learn far more from a reading session when they are doing more than simply listening, but there is no point in spoiling the child's enjoyment of being read to just for a short-term gain. For many young children, the times when they are cuddled up in a warm bed or comfortable chair listening to their parent's voice are the most treasured moments of the day. There is no need to change that. But whenever you read to a young child the situation bristles with learning opportunities. These opportunities fall into several categories.

THE REWARDS OF BEING READ TO

Learning about books

For a start, being read to provides many experiences that will help a child to become an independent reader. Apart from discovering that books provide a marvellous source of knowledge and pleasure, children learn that books are an interesting, entertaining and necessary part of life. Early experience of books gets a young person into the habit of regularly turning to them for information and practical knowledge, as well as recreation.

Listening to stories also helps a child to learn skills that she will need later in order to read herself. Learning how to follow a narrative storyline, remembering events that happened earlier and connecting them to later ones, and discovering how people's motives influence their actions are just some aspects of the enlarged understanding that comes from listening to stories.

Learning about language

Being read to helps a future reader learn some essential facts about written language, many of which have simply not been made available to illiterate adults or children lacking experience of books. Someone who is never exposed to written language may never really understand what words actually *are*. That is because in the language we listen to it isn't always obvious where one word ends and the next one begins. A child with no experience of books may not yet realize that words are made from letters and are organized in sentences and paragraphs. She may not even know that you read from left to right and from top to bottom, and it will not necessarily be clear to her what you do when you get to the end of a page.

For the majority of adults, knowledge of this kind is so familiar that we take it for granted. It is easy to forget that we all once had to learn these basic concepts. Unless a child is given the opportunity to learn about printed words before she starts having reading lessons at school, she will be at a real disadvantage.

Adding to the child's own knowledge

A parent who reads to children adds to their knowledge and understanding. Any child who is read to regularly will have gained a larger vocabulary as a result of coming across lots of new words and unfamiliar expressions. But books do far more than add to children's vocabularies: they provide a window onto all kinds of interesting experiences.

For any young child, the daily routine is inevitably restricted, but books open up new worlds, showing a child all kinds of events and experiences, feeding her imagination with fantasy, adventure, excitement and humour. They make a young person more aware of what it must be like to experience someone else's life, and help her to see things from another person's viewpoint. Stories about other children's hopes and fears help the young to come to terms with their own feelings.

Psychologist Gordon Wells found that of all the activities that contribute to a child becoming literate, the experience of listening to stories is especially valuable. He has also shown that it is easier for young children to assimilate new ideas when they appear within the framework of a story. Even older children find new principles easier to grasp when they are presented in the context of a story or anecdote.

Young children show enormous curiosity and thirst for knowledge, because it is this, above all else, that enables them to make sense of the world they inhabit. Psychologists studying the way in which thinking skills develop have demonstrated that when a young child's understanding is limited or restricted it is usually because she simply lacks the knowledge needed to make something comprehensible. Knowing more means understanding more.

A lack of simple knowledge rather than an absence of thinking skills is often behind children's misunderstandings, and is apparent from the kind of mistakes they make. In the following conversation, quoted by Barbara Tizard and Martin Hughes in *Young Children Learning* [p. 130], the child reaches a conclusion which is wrong.

Child	**Whose party is it?**
Sister	*Franny's Mum and Dad's party.*
Child	**Were Franny's Mum and Dad born on the same day?**

Although the child's conclusion is not correct, it is entirely logical and valid. She knows that people have parties on their birthdays, so she reasons, sensibly enough, that if two people are having a party on the same day, they must have the same birthday. This child does not lack reasoning power – she simply does not know that people can have parties other than on their birthdays.

Reading aloud sessions provide lots of good opportunities for the child to ask questions, and by the age of three or four questions arising from conversations may become one of the child's main ways of exploring. Children in this age group often ask around thirty questions in an hour. These are powerful learning tools as they actively seek new information and explanations, or help a child try to understand something which causes confusion.

Learning to listen

Listening to stories also helps a child to learn to concentrate on the human voice. An individual who cannot do that experiences enormous difficulties in learning to read. Research has shown that children whose parents do not regularly read to them often find it difficult to listen to the *sounds* of words, an essential ability when learning to read.

Children who are not used to attending carefully to the human voice are particularly disadvantaged in the school classroom, where it is important to hear exactly what the teacher is saying. At school there are few opportunities for the non-verbal communications and repetitions of spoken messages that can be relied upon at home.

Having an adult to oneself

Finally, being with a parent who is reading aloud gives a young child valuable time in the company of a calm and attentive adult. For some children a reading session will provide one of the few periods when they have an adult all to themselves. For most, it will be a time that offers good opportunities for practising talking and 'thinking aloud' in the company of someone who is understanding and responsive.

THE ACTIVE LISTENER

There are a number of simple activities that any parent can introduce when reading to a child and which add enormously to the value of that time. That is not to say that we cannot enjoy reading just for the pleasure it brings, and parents do not *always* have to be on the lookout for opportunities for intellectual stimulation. But sometimes it is well worth the effort of making a reading session more than just an experience of passive listening.

It may be easier for your child to take an active role in the reading session if you choose a book with her own experiences and interests in mind. For instance, a book about teddy bears is likely to appeal to a child who enjoys her own teddy. If the child has just taken a trip to see Granny, or a visit to the seaside, a book about the same topic will capitalize on her first-hand experience. Even the experience of everyday shopping will help a child gain more pleasure from books on the subject – we recommend Pat Hutchins' wonderful book *Don't Forget the Bacon*. (Chapter 7 lists plenty of suitable books for young children to enjoy.)

Children's language skills develop greatly when they are encouraged to talk about the stories they are listening to, so aim to get the child talking about the story; the book itself will provide ideas and topics. Although you may have to initiate this by stopping and asking questions, it won't be long before your child talks without prompting. Some children will do this quite spontaneously, without needing any encouragement at all, although that is unusual.

Asking a child questions encourages her to think about the story, and practise expressing her thoughts in words. One question may remind her of a part of the story, and she will try to tell you what she recalls; another question may ask her to anticipate the next part of the story, helping her develop imaginative powers or problem-solving skills. Almost any question will be an invitation to a child to think about something, and also to express thoughts in language. This is an important part of developmental progress, and needs practice.

It is also a good idea to encourage children to ask you questions, and when they do you should *always* be willing to explain. Quite often, there will be items of information in a book that are not at all clear to a young child, and it is important that she feels confident and relaxed about asking for clarification. It is sometimes tempting to say 'Don't interrupt', but if you do that too often the chances are that explanations will be asked for less frequently, and a real learning opportunity is lost. If what your child wants to know is going to become apparent in the next bit of the story, you can suggest that she waits a minute and listens carefully. Then return to the original question to see if subsequent information has answered it.

What kinds of questions are best? Or will any question do? Any query that engages a child's interest and encourages her to express her thoughts in words will be beneficial, but some kinds of questions are more stimulating than others. Look at the following dialogue. Father and son are sitting together, looking at a picture book.

Father	There's a little boy. What colour is his shirt?
Child	**Red.**
Father	Yes, and what is he climbing on?
Child	**Ladder.**
Father	What's at the top of the ladder?
Child	**Pussycat.**
Father	That's right. Is it a big pussycat or a little pussycat?

Here it is clear that the father is doing a conscientious job of asking questions that succeed in getting his child to identify objects in a picture and speak the words out loud. However, the opportunities given to the child to think about the story and express himself through language are rather limited. If you put yourself in the position of the child in the dialogue you will agree that it all seems rather like a test or an examination.

Contrast that dialogue with the following one.

Father	What's the little boy doing?
Child	**Ladder.**
Father	Climbing up a ladder. What's he getting on to, he's on the roof, isn't he? Who's up there, Rosemary? Who's that?
Child	**Pussycat**
Father	Ye . . . es. What's the pussycat doing do you think?
Child	**Jump out.**
Father	Jump out, do you think? Can she jump out? Think the little boy will catch her?
Child	**Yes.**

The adult in the second conversation is just doing what comes naturally to many parents . All the same, he is doing a fine teaching job by helping his child to think and talk about what is going on in the book. As far as the child's awareness is concerned, there is a world of difference between the first conversation and the second one. The father in the first dialogue is, like the parent in the second one, patiently reading to the child, directing her attention to important things in the picture, responding to her statements, and creating some kind of a conversation. Essentially, where this parent is less successful is in not asking questions that really stretch the child's capacity to think and communicate. In the second conversation the child is being encouraged to think about the actions of the participants and anticipate what is going to happen next. She is encouraged to try and see things from the perspective of the characters in the story. The second parent is 'drawing language out' and, unlike the previous dialogue, it really is a conversation, one in which the two partners talk to each other.

The kinds of questions that the second parent asks are similar to those that parents were advised to introduce in a study by Grover Whitehurst and his colleagues. Parents were advised to give their children extra encouragement to talk and think aloud at times when they were reading picture books together. The parents spent less time actually reading, and more time talking, with the child about the stories and the pictures. Although that intervention lasted only for one month there was a very positive outcome with children making real gains in their language skills.

Things to do

- 'What will?', 'What did?', 'How?' and 'Why?' questions are especially helpful ways of encouraging conversation. Obviously, the complexity of a question needs to suit the child's age, but questions like 'Why did the little girl do that?', 'What will happen when she finds out?', 'Why did she cry when he kicked her?' are more likely to encourage language that genuinely expresses ideas in words. Questions that ask for one-word answers, such as 'What colour is the balloon?', 'What do you call that animal?' are not so effective in encouraging a child to express her thoughts in language. Yet there is no need to feel that questions which only need a short answer should be entirely avoided. With very young children there may be no alternative, and short-answer questions can often be a good way to start a conversation or to encourage a child to attend to something interesting.

- It is often helpful to ask the kinds of 'why?' and 'how?' questions that do not have any particular right answer, and to ask a child to make an individual judgement or an imaginative response. Questions which invite a child to say what she thinks are less likely to make her feel she is being tested than those which require a correct answer. Don't worry if a young child misunderstands a 'why?' question at first. It takes time to learn to appreciate precisely what adults mean by 'why?', and your child will gradually reach a fuller understanding of what a 'why?' question is actually requesting.

- Don't worry if at first you find it hard to think of suitable questions. You will find that it is much easier to construct them if you look through a book in advance, when you are on your own and do not have to concentrate on other things. If you still find it difficult, you will find that adapting the questions listed below will produce a number of suitable ones.

'What's happening to the boy in the picture?'
'What is the little girl thinking?'
'What do you think the cat will do?'
'Why is Tom pushing Anna away?'
'What do you think the little dog will do next?'
'Why is the boy running away from the big lion?'
'How do you think she will find her kitten?'
'What will happen if she catches the mouse?'

- Try questions that specifically ask a child how she would act if she were a character in the story; for instance, 'What would you do if you were the farmer?' As well as giving the child practice in imagining she is in someone else's place, they are also helpful in revealing something of the child's thinking and the level of her understanding of a story.

- Be careful not to depend too much on questions that have 'yes' or 'no' answers, such as 'Do you think she's clever?' or 'Is the man wearing a hat?'. Too many of these questions can make a child feel pressurized. This problem does not arise with questions that ask a child for her opinion or judgement, or encourage her to use her imagination.

- Respond positively to what is said, and give feedback that lets a child know her message was received. One way of doing this is to expand on the child's own answers, another is to suggest alternative responses. A nice example of expansion by a parent was included earlier in this chapter:

Father	*Ye . . . es. What's the pussycat doing do you think?*
Child	**Jump out.**
Father	*Jump out, do you think? Can she jump out? Think the little boy will catch her?*

- Be generous with positive and encouraging remarks like 'good' and 'well done'. But don't make the child *too* dependent upon your praise. When she is engaged in an activity she is clearly enjoying, show enthusiasm and encouragement, but allow the child to enjoy the activity for its own sake. A child who is internally motivated in this way will become more independent.

- Make progressive changes as a child's mastery of language increases. That is, start with questions that are easy for the child to understand and answer, and gradually introduce more challenging questions and more complex language.

- Always be willing to explain again and again. The contents of a book may be totally unfamiliar to your child, and unfamiliar things are often difficult to understand. When adults say that a book is 'too difficult' for a child, what they often mean is that it introduces unfamiliar ideas. Children and adults alike are able to 'make sense' of something new only when it can be related to something we already know. It will help your child if you look for ways to form such connections. For instance, when introducing your child to a new book you might say 'This is a book about a postman. Do you we remember we saw a postman yesterday? What was he wearing? What do postmen do? Well, here is a postman in this book . . .'.

- Before you start reading aloud, it is often a good idea for parent and child to talk about the book in general. In this way you can make sure that the child has all the background information that is needed to fit the new material into a familiar context. Usually the pictures on the outside of a book will be helpful. You could say something like 'I wonder what this book is about. What's that in the picture on the cover? Yes, it's a cat, and what is she doing? Yes, and she does look angry, doesn't she. Why do you think that is? Perhaps we'll find out when we read the story'.

- As well as being prepared to provide any necessary explanations before you start on a new story, you should also go on explaining as the book unfolds. It may be that the text gives all the information your child needs in order to understand the story, but you cannot take that for granted. Often, it is worth drawing attention to the information provided by the illustrations which, in many instances, will help a child understand elements of the story that may not be clear from the text alone.

- A children's author writes with the assumption that the child reader (or listener) will already have some of the background knowledge needed to make sense of the story. An author has to strike a balance between giving too little background information, which may mean young readers do not understand the story, or too much, in which case they are likely to find it boring. Achieving the right balance is particularly challenging and, as we have seen, there will often be times when a parent's help is needed to make sense of a new and unfamiliar story.

7 | What Should I Read to my Child?

This chapter gives very practical information about available children's books, from first baby board books to text-only storybooks. The focus here is on those books that you can read to and with your child, rather than books that a child might read independently, although in practice these categories often eventually overlap.

The preceding chapter has already outlined some reasons why it is advantageous for young children to get used to enjoying books from an early age. There is no reason why you can't start using books from the time your baby is around six months of age, although this may seem an odd idea if you have always assumed that books only start to be valuable when a child is already talking. As we have seen, babies develop language from listening to human speech, and because talking to babies can make some parents feel self-conscious, reading or talking about books is a useful way to give an adult something to say – you are, after all, being given your lines.

Dorothy Butler, the author of *Babies Need Books* (published by Pelican) a lovely, stimulating and informative read on the subject, suggests that reading with your child should begin very early.

Here is what one mother has to say about early reading:

I 'read' to Chloe from a very early age. At four months she would sit on my lap and we would enjoy picture board books together.

It was a good way of focusing her attention and it gave me something to talk to her about, describing the brightly drawn animals, turning the pages to another image. She was fascinated, and now at three she has her own little shelf of books, including some pretty tatty early books that she refers to as her 'baby books'. Her books are as important to her as her other toys.

This parent has given her daughter the opportunity to explore books from a very early age, so they now form a natural part of her life. She is familiar with handling them and later will probably not be daunted by the idea of reading.

Over time, as favourite picture books are read and reread, the storylines become memorized. A child seems to 'read' the text, is familiar with the way stories evolve, begins to recognize words in a memorized book and transfers this knowledge elsewhere. All the time, confidence in using books is growing. As we have seen, although reading regularly to children will not actually teach them to read, it does help children to gain skills that make the process of learning to read more easily assimilated. And, perhaps most important of all, early familiarity with books demonstrates to your child that reading opens up a whole world of imagination and fun.

Introducing a peaceful time with a book, perhaps prior to a rest or bedtime, can be a useful way of helping small children to wind down, and will eventually encourage them to sit quietly with a book by themselves. Above all, reading should be an enjoyable pastime, and if you are just beginning to introduce books to a young child that may mean concentrating for only a few minutes at a time.

The lists of books that appear in this chapter give only a general indication of what is appropriate for an age group. As each child is unique, each will approach a new experience in her own individual way, and in her own time. You will know your child better than anyone, and can gauge how she is responding. Keep in mind that these lists are suggestions only: there is no problem in using a book supposedly designed for an older child, if it engages your baby's attention.

BOOKS FOR BABIES

Board books are very popular for use with babies, as they are designed to be visually appealing to this age group, with clear and brightly coloured pictures, little or no text and very simple storylines. The firmness of the board makes them easy for a baby to hold, and less easy to damage. Given that they have to withstand possible chewing and throwing, this is fairly important. There is nothing to stop you using more conventional books written for an older child, but any baby worth its salt is going to make a grab for the pages of a book at some stage.

Bath books, made of brightly illustrated padded plastic, are attractive and make a lovely bath toy. At some point, however, your child will need to differentiate between these and other books, or she might, quite reasonably, think that any book could be used in the bath. Fabric books make great 'in-bed' reading and they can be safely left in the cot for the child to read before or after sleeping. They are useful to pack with a travel cot.

Often board books focus on groups of items, such as clothes, food or toys, with which a baby might be familiar and begin to recognize. Books featuring other babies and people can be successful, for babies respond particularly to faces, even quite crudely drawn face shapes. You will be able to judge what holds your baby's attention, for even a short period, and you can use the same book time and again. There is nothing to stop you making your own book, too, perhaps cutting out colourful pictures from magazines and sticking them in an exercise book.

Look out for the following board books which we think are particularly appealing: *Animals* and *My House* both from the 'My First Chunky Board Books' series published by HarperCollins; Sandra Boynton's *The Going to Bed Book* and *Moo, Baa, LaLaLa* published by Methuen; the *Pooh Board Books* also published by Methuen (look out too for other board books based on classic children's books, such as *Peter Rabbit, Noddy*, etc.); Helen Oxenbury's *Bedtime, Shopping* and *Holidays* are three more from Methuen; Eric Hill (author of the *Spot* books) has also done *The Park* and *Bear at Home*, published by Heinemann. Michelle Cartledge's *Teddy Bear* board books are available from Sainsbury's supermarkets.

Board books, and other children's books, often turn up very cheaply and in good condition at second-hand sales. If you are concerned about giving your baby second-hand books, remember that the majority are laminated and can be wiped clean with a mild disinfectant.

PICTURE BOOKS

Now that you and your baby are established readers, so to speak, the sky is the limit. The wealth and variety of children's books in this next group are tremendous, and you will be spoilt for choice. Although the emphasis remains on the pictures, there is usually a definite storyline, quite short, because a small child's attention span is still limited. Because being read to is about learning to listen and enjoying the rhythm of words, there is often a repetitive element in the simple text of a picture book. It is helpful to have subjects that provide a point of reference in your child's life, with clear pictures that you can talk to her about, encouraging conversation and developing vocabulary. Look for books that you will enjoy reading too.

Look for Janet and Allan Ahlberg's *Peepo!* and *The Baby's Catalogue* (Picture Puffins); John Burningham's *The Blanket* and *The Friend* (Random Century); Eric Hill's *Where's Spot?* and *Spot's First Walk* (Heinemann); Helen Oxenbury's *Pippo* series (Walker Books); Dick Bruna's *Muffy* books (Methuen); and Sarah Garland's *Doing the Washing* and *Going Shopping* (Picture Puffins).

There is a good range of books giving a first introduction to the alphabet and numbers, where the emphasis is largely on providing visual and verbal stimulation. Among these are Helen Oxenbury's *ABC of Things* (Heinemann); Jane Miller's *Farm Alphabet Book* (Dent); Dick Bruna's *U and I Can Count* (Methuen); Eric Carle's *The Very Hungry Caterpillar* (Hamish Hamilton); Gerald Whitcomb's *abc* (Ladybird); Brian Wildsmith's *ABC* (Oxford); Pat Hutchins' *One Hunter* (Puffin) and Molly Bang's *Ten, Nine, Eight* (Julia MacRae).

Nursery rhyme books are a must; the rhythm, rhyming and repetitive nature of nursery rhymes, as well as the narrative make them fun to read, and fun for your child to learn. And rhymes, particularly, encourage a child to listen carefully to the actual sounds of words, which help develop essential listening skills needed when learning to read. Choose from Brian Wildsmith's *Mother Goose* (Oxford); Raymond Briggs' *Mother Goose Treasury* (Puffin); Frank Hampson's *A First Ladybird Book of Nursery Rhymes* (Ladybird); Nicola Bayley's *Book of Nursery Rhymes* (Puffin); *The Faber Book of Nursery Verse* (Faber); and Beatrix Potter's *Apply Dapply's Nursery Rhymes* and *Cecily Parsley's Nursery Rhymes* (F. Warne and Co.), and Elizabeth Matterson's *This Little Puffin* (Puffin).

Often parents find that if they deviate from a familiar text, or if they break off for any reason – perhaps to talk about what is happening – their child will insist on the story continuing as they know it should! This response to a book or books may last for quite a while. Go on introducing others, in addition to the current favourite, and bear with your child's need to keep on going back to the same story – it will pass, although there may always have to be one particular favourite to fall back on at any given time.

Sometimes you may get sick of a book your child loves. As one mother said,

'Much as I loved the simplicity and amusing storyline of Spot, I must have had to read it a hundred times and was heartily sick of it before we eventually moved on. Even now, there are still occasional requests to have it read again, although I think he could just about read it himself!'

This is a very common experience among parents. One consolation is that at least it demonstrates that your child has learned that books are interesting and enjoyable. Other things have been learned, too; she is able to concentrate for a period of time, able to focus on your voice, able to carry the storyline in her head, and able to anticipate what will happen next. These are all useful lessons for future learning.

As your child's language skills develop and her attention span increases, you can introduce more complicated story-lines and more detailed pictures. You will probably find that your child will vary in her choice of books, choosing quite simple ones one day, more complicated ones another. Try *This Is the Bear* by Sarah Hayes, illustrated by Helen Craig (Walker); *Each, Peach, Pear, Plum* by Janet and Allan Ahlberg (Picture Puffins); *Dogger* by Shirley Hughes (Picture Lions); *I Want to See the Moon* by Louis Baum, illustrated by Niki Daly (Magnet); *Harry the Dirty Dog* by Gene Zion, illustrated by Margaret Bloy Graham (Picture Puffins); *The Elephant and the Bad Baby* by Elfrida Vipont, illustrated by Raymond Briggs (Picture Puffins). Countless children have enjoyed Beatrix Potter stories. Although some use quite complex language, this won't necessarily prevent your child from enjoying them. Start with the simpler stories like *The Story of Miss Moppet* and *The Tale of Peter Rabbit* (F. Warne & Co.). Also recommended are *Postman Pat's Difficult Day* by John Cunliffe, illustrated by Celia Berridge and based on the television series (Hippo Books); *Where the Wild Things Are* by Maurice Sendak (Picture Puffins); *Peace at Last* and *Five Minutes Peace* by Jill Murphy (Picture Mac); *Mr Gumpy's Outing* by John Burningham (Picture Puffins); *Old Bear*, *Little Bear's Trousers*, *Little Bear Lost*, and *Jolly Tall* by Jane Hissey (Beaver Books) and *Winnie the Witch* by Valerie Thomas, illustrated by Korky Paul (Oxford).

Books provide a safe window on life's experiences, and can be used to stimulate thought and discussion about something that has happened in your child's life; *Starting School* by Janet and Allan Ahlberg (Puffin), for example, or Shirley Hughes' *Moving Molly* (Random Century), which is about moving house. Then there are picture books like *My Baby Brother* by Harriet Hains (Dorling Kindersley) or *I Am Adopted* by Michael Chapman (Bodley Head), designed to meet specific needs.

Story books are very useful for exploring difficult or troubling aspects of a child's life and there are some that can be used quite deliberately to help explain abstract ideas and make them accessible. Susan Varley's *Badger's Parting Gifts* (Random Century) for example, is a wonderful story that explores the themes of death, grieving and happy memories. Pat Hutchins' *Tom and Sam* (Bodley Head) shows in a very subtle way, how the importance of friendship can override jealousy. Maurice Sendak's *Where the Wild Things Are* (Puffin) demonstrates to small children that they can have some control over both their imaginative fears and angry feelings.

In encouraging your children to enjoy, value and appreciate books it is often a nice idea for a child to have her own bookshelf, within her reach, so she can choose her own book, and put it away afterwards.

USING THE LIBRARY

Visits to the local library can become a regular highlight in a small child's life. Most libraries have a well-arranged children's area, where children of all ages can sit and look at a wide variety of books before making their selection. Children's librarians can be an enormous help in recommending books for different stages, too, and will trace and order books from other libraries if these are not available in their own.

Many libraries organize regular child-centred activities such as weekly storytelling sessions for different age-groups. Often displays are mounted to highlight different types of books (first picture books, multi-racial books, selected books which key into news, sports, or cultural events) or draw attention to book-related activities like Children's Book Week.

Libraries also have supplies of children's pre-recorded audio tapes. (Many bookshops now stock story tapes too, as do outlets like W.H. Smith and Woolworth.) Audio tapes are most useful with children who are already familiar with the process of storytelling and can listen attentively to an unfamiliar voice. Selecting stories with which your child is already familiar, listening together and using tapes in conjunction with the books, is a good way of introducing story tapes. Eventually children can listen to them independently. Tapes are wonderful on car journeys, too, as one parent told us.

We were introduced to the delights of Winnie-the-Pooh, which I had never had as a child, by the story tapes with Alan Bennett reading *The House at Pooh Corner*. He brings it to life beautifully and I enjoy it as much as my son. From this introduction I am now reading the Pooh Bear stories aloud, and I hope eventually he will want to read them for himself.

You might like to record your own story tapes for your child, making a selection of personal favourites. The familiarity of both the stories and your voice may make the tape easier for your child to listen to in the first instance. Or you can both record stories together, enhancing the way in which you are using a story book. You can do this from quite a young age, perhaps starting with an animal story book like *Moo, Baa, LaLaLa* (Methuen) which actively encourages participation:

Rhinoceroses snort and snuff
And little dogs go RUFF RUFF RUFF

Children are often very good at memorizing verses, and you could build on this when creating your own tapes. Take the rhyming couplets in *Each, Peach, Pear, Plum* (Picture Puffins) for example: you and your child could record these, each taking alternate lines:

Each, Peach, Pear, Plum
I spy Tom Thumb
Tom Thumb in the cupboard
I spy Mother Hubbard.

And so on. These are only two suggestions, and provide just a starting point. Audio tapes also make a delightful oral record of your child's progress, and she will probably adore recording her voice.

LONGER BOOKS

By the time a child gets to around five years of age you will probably be looking for books with longer, more complex storylines. Bright, interesting illustrations are still important to enhance the text and clarify the story, but are not so crucial to the narrative.

Here are a few suggestions:

Sam Pig's Trousers and *Sam Pig and the Wind* by Alison Uttley, illustrated by Graham Percy (Faber) are two stories from *The Adventures of Sam Pig* which have been beautifully reissued as individual books; *The Enormous Crocodile* by Roald Dahl, illustrated by Quentin Blake (Puffin); *Fireman Sam and the Bonfire* by Diane Wilmer, one of four titles based on the television series (Heinemann); *The Big Concrete Lorry* by Shirley Hughes (Walker Books); *Alfie Gets in First* by Shirley Hughes (Bodley Head); *The Story of Babar* by Jean de Brunhoff (Methuen); *'Little Tim' Adventures* by Edward Ardizzone (Puffin); *Mrs Pig Gets Cross and Other Stories* and *Crocodarling* by Mary Rayner (Picture Lions); *Thomas the Tank Engine* by the Revd W. Awdry (Kaye & Ward); *Winnie the Pooh* and *The House at Pooh Corner* by A.A. Milne (Mammoth); the newly revised and updated *Noddy* storybooks by Enid Blyton (BBC Books); *The Tailor of Gloucester* by Beatrix Potter (F. Warne & Co.); and *The Selfish Giant* by Oscar Wilde, illustrated by Michael Foreman (Puffin).

Although many of these stories are self-contained, some already break down into chapters, allowing you to read one or more chapters at a time and introducing the idea that a book is not necessarily read all at once. This is quite a sophisticated leap in understanding, and depends on your child being able to retain the content of previous chapters from one day to another. It is always useful to recap briefly before you start a new chapter, although very often she will remember exactly what has happened – probably more so than you.

In between reading longer books, you may find she asks for earlier, simpler picture books. Take her lead on this. The golden rule in introducing more demanding books to children is to do so regularly but without pressure, allowing their ideas of what they enjoy to dictate your pace.

WHAT NEXT?

The next list of suggested books have only occasional line illustrations but are still relatively short overall, and broken down into brief chapters. These are excellent to read from and will probably be included later among those books your child will first read to herself, though it won't spoil her enjoyment if she has heard the story before.

Have a look at the following:
The Hen Who Wouldn't Give Up by Jill Tomlinson (Mammoth); *Little Red Fox* by Alison Uttley (Puffin); *The Magic Finger* by Roald Dahl (Puffin); *The Worst Witch* by Jill Murphy (Puffin); *Josie Smith* by Magdalen Nabb (Young Lions); *Clever Polly and the Stupid Wolf* by Catherine Storr (Puffin); *Mr Majeika* by Humphrey Carpenter (Puffin); and *Teddy Robinson* by Joan G Robinson (Puffin). These books all form part of a larger series so once you and your child have discovered and enjoyed these, there are more to come.

NOVELTY BOOKS

A fairly recent innovation in children's book publishing is the large number of novelty books – pop-ups, lift-the-flap, touch-and-feel – published each year, usually around Christmas time. Some are undoubtedly exceptionally well thought out and constructed, but they all run a greater than average risk of getting damaged, and it is wise to consider carefully whether your child will be able to handle it effectively.

The age range of novelty books is wide, from the very simple lift-the-flap books for little fingers, like Rod Campbell's *Dear Zoo* (Puffin), to the much more complicated paper engineering of something like *Watch it Work: The Plane* by Ray Marshall and John Bradley (Viking Kestrel). Others worth considering include *Sam's Sandwich* by David Pelham (Random Century); *Dinosaurs in Action* and *Sharks in Action* (Childs Play); *The Jolly Postman* by Janet and Allan Ahlberg (Heinemann); *Dinner with Mr Fox* by Stephen Wylie and Korky Paul (Orchard) and *Mrs Wolf* by Shen Roddie and Korky Paul (Tango Books); *The Car and Truck* by Gerard Browne (Orchard Books); *Wings: A Pop-Up Book of Flight* by Nick Bantock (Bodley Head); and *A Christmas Carol* by Charles Dickens (Orchard Books).

FIRST READERS

Your child may begin to 'read' her favourite books to you; initially this will mean memorizing the text, perhaps introducing other words as well. If she does this, you will obviously want to give her the confidence to continue, and find books that encourage the process. Many of a child's first picture books can be reused like this, even if it means digging them out again. There is a chance that they will be rejected as not 'proper' reading books, although this is more likely once your child has started school and seen what books are used there for learning to read.

Reverting to a simpler story may seem rather boring if your child is now used to having quite sophisticated stories read aloud. Some children want to read complicated books straight away, and are put off by the simplicity of those books they can actually manage. If this is the case, you will have to be particularly tactful, or not bother with books in your existing repertoire at all.

There are series of books that have been carefully designed for a child learning to read, which are often referred to as 'reading schemes'. Modern reading schemes are much livelier than the 'Janet and John' you might remember, with more interesting stories and less repetitive use of key words. Text is very clearly set in upper and lower case letters, with minimum punctuation. This is to identify clearly word shapes and letters, but the text is not so large as to distort the word shapes so they appear to run one into another.

Puffin have two series, *Hello Reading* and *I Can Read*, each with the emphasis on bright and interesting storylines. Usborne Publishers have a well-devised series called *Usborne Farmyard Tales*, which can be used purely as picture books or as first readers. Ladybird's *Read With Me* series includes notes on how to use the books to encourage your child, and there are also activity books that tie in with the reading books.

AND, FINALLY . . .

Many parents wonder when they should stop reading to their children. There is no particular age: many children enjoy being read to long after they are competent readers themselves, and having a story read aloud, perhaps before bed, remains a cherished part of family life. Even when your child is reading well, perhaps reading those books that you had previously read to them, there are others that may still be outside their capabilities, but they would love to hear anyway. This last list includes many books your child will probably read to herself eventually, but will not be spoilt by having been read aloud in the first instance.

Charlotte's Web by E.B. White (Puffin); *Finn Family Moomintroll* by Tove Jansson (Puffin); *Adventures of the Little Wooden Horse* by Ursula Moray Williams (Puffin); *Nurse Matilda* by Christianna Brand (Knight); *Charlie and the Chocolate Factory* by Roald Dahl, also *Esio Trot* and *The BFG* and others (Puffin); *The Complete Chronicles of Narnia* by C.S. Lewis (Lion); *The Wolves of Willoughby Chase* by Joan Aiken (Puffin); *The Little Prince* by Antoine de Saint-Exupéry (Piccolo); *The Borrowers* by Mary Norton (Puffin); *Little House on the Prairie* by Laura Ingalls Wilder (Puffin); *The Incredible Adventures of Professor Branestawm* by Norman Hunter (Puffin); *Ramona the Pest* by Beverly Clearly (Puffin); and *The Hobbit* by J.R.R. Tolkien (HarperCollins).

SOME CHILDREN'S BOOK CLUBS

Puffin Book Club
27 Wrights Lane
London W8 5TZ   071 938 2200

Books For Children
PO Box 70
Cirencester
Gloucester GL7 AZ   0793 420 000

Scholastic Book Clubs
Westfield Road
Southam
Leamington Spa
Warwickshire CV33 OJH   0926 813 910

The Red House
Witney
Oxfordshire OX8 5YF   0993 779 090

The Bookworm Club
20 Trinity Street
Cambridge CB2 3NG   0223 358 351

Letterbox Library
Second Floor
Leroy House
436 Essex Road
London N1 3QP   071 226 1633

8 | Getting Ready for Learning to Read

Like many of a child's achievements, learning to read is helped enormously by opportunities and incentives encountered in everyday family life. The availability of these makes a huge difference for a child. In Switzerland, many children are good skiers at five, because learning to ski is part of the culture. At the same age, youngsters growing up in the Manu tribe of New Guinea, who live in houses set on stilts above tidal lagoons, are expert at controlling a canoe. They are also good swimmers, as are the majority of five year olds throughout the world who are lucky enough to live in homes that have a swimming pool. In environments such as these young children readily gain impressive skills, simply because they happen to grow up where there are strong opportunities and incentives to learn, and where the skills form a natural part of daily life. Reading is no exception. The same advantages are conveyed by being made aware of the benefits of reading and by having frequent opportunities to learn how to do it.

But learning to read is a major achievement and in order to read a book a child needs a number of interlocking skills. Failure to acquire any of these can lead to reading problems. There are a number of ways in which difficulties can arise, and when a child does not happen to find reading easy it is important not to rush to conclude that there must be something seriously wrong.

In this chapter we describe a variety of practical things

you can do to help prepare a child to learn to read. Two of the most important influences have already been mentioned. The first is the child's own skill with spoken language. Children whose language skills are good have far fewer reading problems than children with poor language skills. The second significant influence is the child's experience of being read to. There is firm evidence that children whose parents regularly read to them have fewer reading problems than those whose parents do not.

FUNDAMENTAL SKILLS

Children who have a good mastery of their own language have already gained some of the skills that a reader needs to depend upon. Yet it is possible that a child who is not regularly read to, although seeming to have an adequate command of spoken language, may fail to gain certain key language skills needed to make satisfactory progress with reading.

Researchers Peter Bryant and Lynette Bradley discovered that one cause of problems with learning to read in a substantial number of children is that they cannot tell similar letter sounds apart. These children are poor at perceiving the smallest sound units of language. When they are trying to learn to read they experience enormous difficulties because reading is practically impossible unless the person can hear language accurately enough to distinguish between similar sounds such as the *b* in bad and the *d* in dad.

These researchers asked four and five year olds to listen to lists containing three words. In two of the words there was a sound in common. For example, one list was *dig dot bun*. The child had to say which was the odd word out. When the same children were tested at reading and spelling four years later, those who did well at this task were usually found to perform adequately. But those children who were initially less competent at the three word exercises tended to be poor readers.

The next stage of this investigation involved selecting young children who had done poorly at the original task, and who therefore seemed to be 'at risk' as far as reading was concerned. Some of these four and five year olds were given special training to help them learn to tell similar letter sounds apart. The children were tested again when they were eight years old. By this time those who had done poorly at the original task and had not been given any special training afterwards were lagging a year behind the standard of achievement at reading and spelling considered normal. But the children who had been taught to discriminate between letter sounds were reading at the normal level for their age. It is clear that helping them to learn a specific skill they previously lacked had prevented serious reading difficulties arising in future years.

Before you rush off to give your child special training at discriminating between letter sounds, be reassured that if she has good language skills she will almost certainly be capable of telling word and letter sounds apart. Provided that parents regularly read to them, children will gain the basic language skills that reading depends on without requiring any special instruction. It helps if there are opportunities to enjoy rhyming games and other activities that involve carefully attending to words and their sounds. The only children who are likely to be at risk are those who have not had opportunities to listen to stories and rhymes.

ESSENTIAL LANGUAGE EXPERIENCES

So children need to have a good mastery of basic language, and parents who regularly talk with them and read stories to them. What else do children need in order to minimize difficulties in learning to read? Three major requirements are outlined here, and the *Things To Do* section that follows describes games and play activities which will help your child acquire prereading skills.

First, it is important for a child to grow up in an environment that is rich in printed or written materials, where she can experience how reading contributes to people's lives, as a source of both entertainment and practical information.

Imagine your daily routine. You get up, brush your teeth and wash, go downstairs and locate the marmalade and a cereal packet, and perhaps turn on the television or radio for the news. Even in this short time, you could explain the meaning of the words on the toothpaste tube to your child, or help her to understand how the words on a jar of marmalade provide information about the contents. You might encourage her to identify some of the simpler words, locating ones that appear in more than one place. Watch out for words to appear on the TV screen. Encourage your child to appreciate the important information that words convey. For instance, if you are looking at the newspaper to find out when a television programme begins, share this activity by showing your child what you are doing, and why. Almost every home is potentially rich in opportunities for your child to become familiar with words and letters, and aware of the enormous benefits gained by being able to interpret them. The parent's job is to ensure that the potential opportunities become real ones. You can do this by sharing with your child some of the numerous occasions on which you rely on reading.

The second feature of a home environment that helps children learn to read more easily is that it provides opportunities for them to see that family members read regularly and enjoy doing so. Look for ways to show your child that you enjoy reading and employ your reading skills for purposes other than the strictly practical. Share something funny you have read in a newspaper or magazine. If you are a habitual book reader, show how much you like reading, so that children really grasp what it means to you.

It is possible that your child may think of reading as something that is fun for adults but not for children. You might counter this by showing how books can give access to knowledge about topics in which he is interested. Children's questions often provide opportunities for you to demonstrate the practical value of reading by looking up information in a book.

Avoid giving the impression that reading is a pastime which you keep to yourself. Try to make a positive response to any questions about your own reading or any expression of interest. A friend recently lent one of us her copy of Christopher Green's book *Toddler Taming*, which has many lively cartoon pictures of toddlers and their parents. It was good to see that the owner's child had coloured in many of the pictures and added extra features of her own. This was a splendid manifestation of parent and child sharing their enjoyment of a book, but you may need to make it clear to yours that only some books are suitable for this kind of treatment!

The third variety of prereading skills needed includes the ability to recognize letters and a few simple words, and being able to write single letters. There are numerous games and play activities that will provide opportunities for prereading skills to be learned and practised, and we make some suggestions in the Things to Do section: amongst these, you might try placing word labels upon familiar objects, and using flash cards.

Yet if a child is not broadly encouraged to enjoy what reading offers, the unimaginative use of flash cards and similar materials may do little to engage her interest. Simply having a label that says 'FRIDGE' stuck on the refrigerator door will not accomplish very much, unless there are plenty of genuine opportunities for a child to identify the word and match it with the object.

SHOULD I TEACH MY CHILD TO READ?

Some language experts believe that it is wrong to teach a preschool child to read. They give a number of reasons: one is the danger of placing too much pressure on a young child. A second is the likelihood that a child who is well-prepared for reading and keen to learn will make faster progress at around five years than at a younger age. Another claim is that since reading is a difficult compound skill, teaching it effectively requires teachers who have knowledge and technical skills that most parents do not possess. Once a parent's teaching becomes at all formal or structured, there is thought to be a risk that a child may be confused by differences between teaching methods used at home and school.

There are undoubtedly some advantages in learning to read early. Reading can make a child more independent and self-sufficient. Instead of having to rely on an adult for decoding all the interesting information that is contained in books, the young reader can start to do this on her own. Investigations that have looked at the ways in which children are affected by learning to read earlier than usual have reached varying conclusions, but there is no doubt that some children have gained real benefits as a result of being able to read at an unusually young age.

There are also possible disadvantages, in addition to the ones already mentioned. A child whose parents encourage too strongly may start to fear, perhaps with justification, that once he can read on his own those cosy sessions of bedtime reading with Mum or Dad will diminish. A child who is already reading when he begins school may suffer from being out of step with other children. And although learning to read early *can* bring real advantages, there is no guarantee that it always *will*. You cannot be sure that a young child who has succeeded in learning to read as a result of intensive parental teaching will actually enjoy reading. She may be too weakly motivated to make any genuine use of her reading skills.

On the other hand, not all the arguments against teaching reading to preschool children are entirely convincing. Take, for instance, the familiar claim that because reading is so complex a skill it is essential that it be taught by a qualified teacher with expert knowledge about the 'correct' way to teach it. If that assertion were entirely true it would be hard to understand why a substantial number of motivated youngsters do manage to learn to read, largely by their own efforts, with no formal teaching from anyone and only a modest amount of help from their parents.

Methods of teaching reading

Educators do not agree among themselves about the best ways to teach reading, so it is understandable that the issue is one that generates confusion. It is widely but incorrectly believed that there are two distinct methods of teaching. In one method, 'phonics', a child learns to decode words by discovering how they are made up from smaller sound units. In the 'look and say' method, alternatively known as the 'whole word' or 'sight' approach, the child learns to identify whole words.

In fact, phonics and look and say are not distinct teaching methods. It is more realistic to regard them as being two kinds of approaches to reading words, each of which has a necessary role in learning to read. These days, most approaches to reading involve both phonics and look and say components.

A child given instruction in phonics learns how words are constructed from sounds, finding out how to identify what letters correspond to which sounds, and establishing the sounds of which a word consists. In other words, the beginning reader will have learned to 'decode' written language.

Yet in practice, it does not make sense to rely entirely on phonics. One reason is that letter-sound correspondences are often irregular, especially in English. For instance, *ow* has different sounds in *cow* and *tow*, and *ou* sounds different in *cough, rough* and *round*. These irregularities often make it impossible to decide how letter combinations sound simply by applying a rule. And the young learner who relied on phonics alone would make very slow progress, becoming discouraged. To prevent this, most teachers favour teaching beginning readers to identify a number of words by the look and say approach, enabling the child to gain a basic reading vocabulary of common words. Early progress is made faster and easier, because she does not have to decode the sound of every single word that she reads.

The fact that it is not a good idea to rely entirely on phonics does not, however, provide grounds for thinking that phonics can be dispensed with. Without knowledge of phonics, a child may fail to learn the rules about the construction of words that all readers need to internalize, and she is more likely to be a poor speller. Unfortunately, because in the early stages progress at phonics-based learning can seem protracted and difficult for some children, there is a tendency for slower learners to receive less phonics instruction than is necessary, and this may add to their problems in the long run.

As a child's reading skills develop, the contributions of phonic and look and say elements change and intertwine.

For example, as familiarity with the spelling of words increases, a word that was initially read by a process of deliberate decoding (phonics) becomes part of the child's permanent memory bank, and that word can eventually be recognized immediately. And so a child's vocabulary of words recognized at sight increases.

Another kind of knowledge that children acquire and use when they are learning to read is of the letter structures that are encountered in words. If you can already read *light* and *might* and *sight* and then for the first time in your life come across *tight*, you will have a fairly good idea of how to pronounce it. You can reason that if the letters *ight* create a certain sound in one word, the chances are they will have a similar sound in another. Of course, that is not always true, but it is so more often than not. Children as well as adults make use of this kind of knowledge when they are reading. They make analogies from words that they do know in order to make intelligent guesses about the probable sounds of letter sequences they are not so sure about.

So reading skills involve decoding words (phonics), identifying them from memory (look and say), and recognizing similarities with words that are already familiar. The reading process is also influenced by the fact that readers can make predictions about what is coming next. They make guesses and form hypotheses that aid their understanding. A child learning to read will be encouraged to use picture clues and her conceptual awareness to help her discover what an unfamiliar word may be.

To give a simple example, if you encounter the word ELEPHANT in a story, the chances of your correctly identifying that word do not depend entirely on your ability to recognize it (look and say) or decode it (phonics), because useful extra clues will have been given by the context in which the word occurs. The person who reads 'The charging

— raised its trunk' can be fairly sure that the missing word refers to something that charges. That narrows things down a lot. Someone whose phonic skills are sufficient for them to decode the first two letters will be well on the way towards identifying the whole word correctly.

After this discussion, you may feel there are grounds for taking some notice of the 'leave it to the experts' viewpoint. It is, however, worth noting that there is no solid evidence that children who learn to read at home experience more reading problems later in life than children who learn at school.

As will now be apparent, there is no one right answer to the difficult question of whether or not a parent should teach a child to read. It largely depends on the particular child. By far the most important thing parents can do is to make sure that their child is well prepared for reading, which will undoubtedly be of benefit to her. In comparison, it is less certain what children actually gain by learning to read before starting school.

In most circumstances it would be wrong actively to discourage your child from trying to learn to read. It is a good idea to give help and encouragement (but little or no formal instruction) if she is genuinely keen to learn to read, and if she can move ahead under her own steam, having acquired the skills described in this chapter. But there is absolutely nothing to worry about if your preschool child is not yet enthusiastic about reading on her own.

Things to do

The importance of a print-rich environment has already been stressed. Here are some activities designed to ensure that your child has plenty of opportunities to become aware of the importance of printed materials and reading in everyday life. Always remember that when your child gets tired of a game or is bored with it, the best thing to do is to abandon it for the time being. Keep games light-hearted, and if you or your child want to alter a game or invent a new one, go ahead. The aim is here to give you ideas about the *kinds* of activities that have been found to work well; rather than provide an 'approved list' of specified activities that you must undertake.

Whenever you do anything which involves or depends upon reading, share the experience with a child. For example, if you are looking up a phone number in the telephone book, explain to your child how you are using the written symbols in order to discover what you need to do. Show her the digits in the book and on the telephone itself. If you make a habit of doing this whenever you make use of written information, your child will discover for herself that reading is an ordinary but important part of daily life.

Step by step instructions, such as those to be found with kits, assembly furniture, games and activity books, offer ways of showing your child how important reading is to everyday life. You might say 'Let's find how we put this together. Here are the instructions. What do we do first. They start at the top. Oh yes, this says . . .'. If you say something like 'Let's follow the instructions step by step' and then demonstrate how you start at the beginning and progress downwards you will help the child to understand the linear nature of text.

Sometimes it is useful to talk aloud about things you normally take for granted and do not have to think about. Remember that although you know that printed writing goes from left to right and then down the page when we reach the end of a line, this is something that your child has to learn. Try to imagine just how a page of text might appear to a complete non-reader: it would probably look like a block of meaningless shapes and lines, with no clues about the order in which it has to be followed.

Letter games for three to five year olds

It takes time for a child to learn to discriminate and identify all twenty-six letters in the alphabet. The task is made more difficult by the fact that capital and lower case versions of a letter are often very different. Concentrate on lower case letters at first, although right from the beginning it will be useful for your child to know a few capitals, such as the first letter of her own name. Most children find that capital letters are easier to write than lower case letters, because there are more straight lines. Don't be in too much of a hurry for her to learn all the letters.

There are many letter games you and your child will enjoy playing. Both magnetic and wooden letters are useful (you can get ones that slide into wooden blocks, forming the alphabet). It is also a good idea to make a collection of letters written on cards. Note that it is easier for a child to discriminate between letters than to identify single letters.

- For your child's very first letter games you might try mixing up, say, six plastic **m**s and six plastic **t**s and then take out a **t** from the pile and tell your child to find another **t**.
- From that you can progress to a sorting game, in which the child places the **m**s and the **t**s in separate piles.
- Letter pointing games are fun. You simply say the sound and the child points to a letter. Most children find it easier to point to a letter after you have made the letter sound than to specify the sound of a letter you are pointing to, but both kinds of challenge should be incorporated into your games.

- You can make a game more difficult by having a larger number of different letters. Eventually, your child will be able to match or sort all the letters in the alphabet, but she will need to build up to this gradually. Be patient if progress is slower than you think it should be, and if your child does not want to play, leave the activity and try again another time.

There is no need to keep to letter games with a rigid format. Children enjoy switching to fresh challenges quite often. In a five minute period, you might start by asking your child to identify three or four letters with which she is already familiar, and then change to a game in which she looks through a story book for examples of a particular letter. After a minute or two of doing that you might introduce a new letter, perhaps one she has already seen in a letter-sorting game. If your child is beginning to get restless by now, you might decide that the time has come to move to an entirely different activity.

- There are a number of picture books for young children in which the authors draw attention to single letters and find ways of making them interesting. The 'Letter-land' series (Thomas Nelson), for example, is fun for parents and children.
- A child who has had plenty of practice at sorting and matching letters will be well on the way to being able to identify them according to their sounds. Introduce the letter sounds as they are heard in speech.
- When you and your child are looking together at books with words and pictures, draw attention to particular letters from time to time. (Don't spend too long doing this, and don't make it seem like a lesson.) Start with just one letter, and introduce new ones gradually, concentrating on one letter per session at first.

On the whole, young children find consonants easier than vowels, but don't feel that you have to work your way through all the consonants before you introduce any vowels.

Remember to keep things informal, and don't forget to switch to something different when your child shows signs of getting tired of a particular letter game. Give plenty of praise and encouragement, especially when she is finding things difficult. Remember, there is no rush: do not try to press ahead too fast.

Word games

Although reading is by no means solely a matter of recognizing words, being able to recognize a few simple words does help the young reader. It gives a child a useful 'starting' vocabulary, so that it is not essential to work at every single word in a new story, and she will feel more confident if she knows that at least some of the words she comes across in a new story will already be familiar.

- For a very simple word game, have a small pack of cards on each of which is written an action word (walk, jump, run, turn, dance, bend, nod, shake). Each player has to take a card at random and then do the action stated on the card.
- You can also make a game of 'Word Bingo'. Have large cards on which you first draw a four by four grid, and then write a word in each of the sixteen squares. Then make sixteen small cards, with one of the words on each. Each player is given one of the large cards, and takes turns picking one of the small words from a bag or box. Each time a player picks a word that appears on his large card he puts a counter over the word on the card. The first player to get a complete line is the

winner. For a longer game, the winner is the first player to complete his card.

- 'Opposites' is another game to help word recognition. Take twelve pieces of card and mark the back of each pair of them in one of six different colours. On the two cards of each colour write words that are opposites: big/little; up/down; in/out; on/off; under/over; high/low. Then put the cards, word up, on a table. The object of the game is to match the opposites. To check whether she is correct, the child simply turns the cards over to see if they are marked in the same colour.

- 'Shopping lists'. This is similar to 'Opposites'. On one side of various pieces of card write simple shopping word items ('jam', 'eggs', 'bread' 'plums', 'cheese', etc.) and on the other side have a picture showing each item. Before you start playing, you will need to make sure that the child knows which object each picture depicts. Then, when the cards have the words upwards, ask for an item you want. Parent and child can take turns. (As in most games, it helps if parents make a few mistakes!)

- 'Robot talking'. This is a good game for helping your child to understand how words are made out of syllables. It also encourages careful attention to how words sound. The idea is that you pretend to be robots, and you demonstrate how this is done by speaking in a machine-like way, with the same degree of emphasis on every syllable and the same gap between each syllable: 'I am a ro bot. Pass me the mar ma lade. Why are you laugh ing, don't be si lly. Ro bots have won der ful adven- tures every where in the un i verse.' Your child will quickly get the hang of having conversations in robot language.

- 'Definitions'. Child psychologist Allyssa McCabe de- scribes a delightful game which will give your child practice in defining words in a simple way. You have a glove puppet you call Maria the Martian. Coming from Mars, Maria does not know what earthly objects are for and wants to find out about them, so she goes round the room asking about things. 'What is this? A shoe? What's that, what are shoes for?' This game will give your child lots of practice in defining words, explaining what things are for and how they operate.

- Games in which participants think of a word which begins with a certain letter will be fun for a child who is beginning to connect letter sounds to words. You can make things easier by giving clues, or vary the game by specifying particular kinds of words, for example, 'Think of an animal which begins with . . .'.

- Times when your child is 'helping' you in the kitchen provide good learning opportunities, and if your child has not come across a recipe before, you should be prepared to do some explaining. Start by saying what a recipe is: 'A recipe shows us how to make a cake. It tells us all the different things we need to have in order to make the cake and then it tells us what we do with them.' Be careful not to overwhelm a child with too much new information all at once. You can point out particular letters or words, ones that may be already familiar, or ones that are important in the recipe and occur again and again, for example, 'add' and 'mix'. If your child is already learning letters this may be a good opportunity to encourage letter 'spotting'. Read out the list of ingredients before you both start to collect them together. Sometimes there will be opportunities to match up the words on the packets ('flour', 'sugar', etc.) with those in the list of ingredients. At first you can point out the identical words, but your child will soon be able to match the words on her own. The thrill of discovering that written words really can be used for a practical purpose is an excellent learning experience. Then you can make the dish according to the instructions provided in the recipe, so she sees how words are used to help make something.

Rhyming games

As we saw in earlier chapters, rhymes are particularly effective for encouraging a child to listen carefully to the sounds of words and continue to be useful as you build up pre-reading skills. The *Dr Seuss* books are especially strong on rhyming and appeal to three to five year olds. Children usually enjoy even the simplest rhyming games.

- You can start simply by saying 'Sun rhymes with fun. What other words rhyme with fun? What rhymes with gold? What rhymes with old?' Other good words for rhyming are 'cat', 'mice', 'hot', 'pear', 'nut', 'man', 'cook', 'hen'. When you are reading aloud, seize opportunities to draw attention to words that rhyme.
- One simple rhyming game involves parent and child taking turns to provide a word. For example, the child says 'rat', you say 'mat' and the child says 'cat'. You may need to help your child by giving prompts. Imagine she starts with 'bear', you say 'tear' and then the child can't think of another word. You might provide a clue by saying 'Think of a fruit that sounds like tear', and if that it not enough to elicit 'pear' you could sound the first letter or say 'It's a bit like an apple'.
- If your child finds it difficult to think of rhyming words, there are some even simpler rhyming games that may help to get her started. For instance, try reciting familiar poems or nursery rhymes but leave the last word in the line for the child to supply. Or think

of silly mistakes that the child will enjoy correcting: '. . . And frightened Miss Muffett abracadabra'. Or make up a short list of words in which all but one rhyme, and ask your child to listen as you recite the words, telling you which is the odd one out.

Early writing activities from three years onwards

Learning to write takes lots of time and practice. Writing requires fine motor control, and children do not achieve this without having developed adequate muscle control and hand-eye coordination — skills they will have acquired through activities such as sorting, fitting, scribbling, drawing, learning to handle a knife and fork, and so on. It is possible to learn to read without being able to write, but from the time when your child starts to become interested in letters and words it is a good idea to make sure that the child has plenty of opportunities to practise writing. Allow her to experiment by scribbling, which will help her learn to manipulate a pen fluently. Eventually you will see deliberate shapes emerging from the scribbles, identifiable as the earliest stages of writing.

Even before they 'know' their letters, many young children will engage in pretend writing activities in order to make 'a note to Granny' or a 'special' shopping list to complement Mummy's. This kind of emergent writing behaviour goes hand in hand with the emergent reading activities of a child who is becoming aware of the importance of literacy.

- Make sure that writing materials are always available, and choose writing implements that are easy to use. Remember that learning to write is a long and slow process. Be patient, encourage your child's efforts, however imperfect they are, and never allow your child to feel that she has failed. Learning to write can be frustrating, so don't try to supervise too closely, and don't assume that all errors have to be corrected. There is no hurry! Concentrate on making sure that your child gets plenty of opportunities to build up her writing skills gradually.

- At first, copying letters will be too difficult without considerable help, and it is a good idea to have the child draw over letters that you have prepared yourself. These should be large, and thickly lined. Start with a few simple letters at first, and build up gradually.

- As soon as your child's efforts to draw letters start to become at all accurate, it is a good idea to show her the 'correct' way to draw each letter. This advice might seem to contradict what we have said about avoiding a formal approach to learning, but in this particular case your child should start off making letter strokes in the

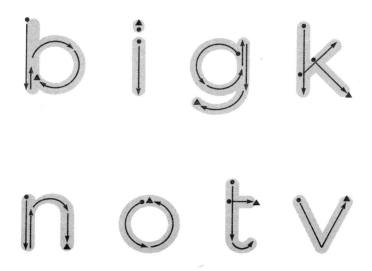

appropriate directions, for it will save frustration in the long run. In the list of letters illustrated here, arrows show the direction in which the pen should be moved, with each letter starting at the dot and finishing at the triangle.

- Once your child knows her letters she can write a shopping list, with you telling her each letter of the word.

9 | Learning about Numbers

With elementary number skills, as with language, a small amount of enjoyable effort on your part can make an enormous difference to your child's progress.

Many children start reciting numbers at two or three years of age, but it may take quite a time for a young learner to use these numbers for real *counting* – assessing how many bricks she has used to build a castle, for example. There is a big difference for a child between simply being able to remember number labels ('one', 'two', 'three', and so on) and understanding the abstract idea that numbers relate not just to particular things but to quantities in general. Even with the simplest number skills, there is more for a child to learn than there appears to be.

FIRST STEPS IN COUNTING AND ADDING

Children master the concept of counting sooner or later, but it needs lots of practical experience to become securely established. That may not happen until long after your child first rattled off 'one, two, three, four'. Giving children plenty of varied and concrete experiences with different quantities of real objects will help them to become familiar with using numbers – the more opportunities the better.

Early learning about numbers and quantities should involve actual objects, or pictures of them. Objects that a child can touch as well as see are particularly helpful. Even when a child starts to add numbers correctly, her thinking will be linked to tangible objects that are added together: the ability to think in abstract terms comes later. You should not be surprised if a child who correctly answers your question about the sum of two tomatoes plus three tomatoes with 'five tomatoes', may fail to answer the question 'What is two plus three?'. She may even ask you what it is you have three of and two of. If you tell her, the chances are that she will then be able to answer correctly.

Eventually your child will understand that two plus two is always four, and six minus one is always five, for example. But that understanding will not arrive until she has had numerous opportunities to discover that when you put two objects together with two more, and then count them all, you now have four objects. She has to discover for herself that this is not only true for, say, apples, but also for eggs, or frogs, or houses, or balls, or any other items.

When you see a child use her fingers for counting, this may be a sign that she has made a big leap towards understanding that you can *represent* objects with other objects. From here it is not far to the stage at which a child can begin to appreciate the idea of a symbol – a number – and that is the key to being able to do arithmetic.

With early number problems your child's answers will often be incorrect, and you will need lots of patience. Sometimes children forget the things that they could do yesterday. When that happens be careful not to react in a way that your child might interpret as being critical. You will have to be especially understanding when your child fails to understand something that seems to you to be obvious or easy, which often happens.

If you detect that a child is getting frustrated at being unable to solve a number task, backtrack a little to an easier problem, so that she feels reassured. If a child finds the right answer on most occasions she will not be too upset if she is occasionally wrong. If she is incorrect more often than she is right, however, she may start to think that she is failing to meet your expectations. In these circumstances a young child can all too easily begin to feel that she is being pushed. Don't hurry your child, and don't try too hard to control things if she is not as cooperative as you would like.

Sometimes the child's priorities will be very different from yours. For your three year old this morning, there are other things she would prefer to do with the toy bricks you would like her to count. Let her follow her inclinations: you can always return to counting later. Even when your child is enthusiastic about the learning activity you introduce, don't persist in it beyond the point where she loses interest or gets distracted. Learning experiences involving numbers and counting can be effective even when they are extremely short. A number of thirty-second counting sessions spread throughout the day will add up to some useful progress.

Occasionally, a conscientious parent who wants to be as encouraging as possible may react *too* enthusiastically to a child's correct answers, with the result that so much importance is attached to getting everything right that the child is upset whenever she is incorrect. You can avoid that happening by taking care not to give too extreme a reaction every single time your child gets something right.

In general, though, with a new and unfamiliar activity it is a good idea for parents to be fairly lavish with praise and encouragement. Once a stage has been reached at which the activity can be enjoyed for its own sake your words of encouragement can become less frequent. Parental praise is always welcome, but too much of it can inhibit a child's independence. As your youngster starts to enjoy an activity more and more for its own sake, you will gradually 'wean' her from her need for constant praise. But don't do that too suddenly.

Introduce number games into everyday activities. They will help a child to understand the practical uses of numbers. Setting the table, weighing things, shopping, cooking from a recipe all provide opportunities for you to share numerical concepts in everyday tasks at home. Psychologists Barbara Tizard and Martin Hughes witnessed a variety of conversations about shopping between mothers and their four year old daughters. In most of these conversations the mother had no educational intent in mind, but it is clear that the child found it beneficial. Part of one conversation went as follows:

Mother	*No, I haven't got enough to get my shopping. All of it.*
Child	**Not all of it?**
Mother	*Irenes just taken five pounds. She'll bring some change back. If she's got some, she'll bring some change back. It's not enough to get all that. Is it? [points to the shopping list]*
Child	**No.**
Mother	*See? So when Daddy gets paid I'll get some more money and then I'll go and get the rest.*
Child	**Yeah. That's nice, isn't it, Mum?**
Mother	*Mm . . . I got one, two, three, four, five, six, seven, eight, nine, ten, eleven, twelve [counts items on list].*
Child	**[Joins in counting] Nine, ten, eleven.**

As Tizard and Hughes observed, this child was learning about counting, and she was also learning some basic practical facts about the ways in which numbers are important in shopping. She was finding out that planning and foresight are needed and that making a written list is a useful way of organizing information. She was discovering that the number of items to be bought has to be balanced against the amount of money available. She may also have gained some understanding of what people can buy with a sum like five pounds.

Most children enjoy counting, perhaps because it gives

them a sense of mastery and control over objects, and many enjoy practising their number skills. Some children will count small toys and other everyday objects quite spontaneously, just as a routine play activity. In order to cope with basic arithmetic a child will also need to be familiar with concepts such as more/less, up/down, long/short, above/below, light/heavy, thick/thin. Knowing about different shapes is also helpful. Not all children who have learned to count will have gained a good understanding of these dimensions, and it is useful if they have some grasp of such things.

TIME

Time is another important concept that is related to numbers and quantities. Don't be worried if your child finds the idea of time difficult to comprehend. Even when they begin school, some children's understanding of time is very limited. Teachers often find young children asking, a short time after they have arrived for the day, whether they have had their lunch, or whether it is time to go home.

Knowing about time is important not only for its part in numerical understanding – a sense of time contributes to a child's social and emotional awareness, and helps her to see the importance of making plans and having long-term goals. A youngster who lacks any real understanding of the future and the past may even find it hard to maintain a sense of identity or experience a feeling of being in control of her life.

Various kinds of experience contribute to a young child's understanding of time. For instance, a child aged three or four who regularly listens to stories will become familiar with the meanings of words such as before/after, earlier/later, young/old, yesterday/today/tomorrow. Opportunities to learn about growing plants will help introduce a child to concepts like weeks and months, though a four year old will still probably have a very vague notion of the difference between such periods.

When should you start teaching your child to tell the time? That depends upon the individual child, but like most other achievements, start by building upon what she already knows. Practical information on teaching a child to tell the time is given on page 119. Before you start, your child will need to be able to count to twelve, have some understanding of how days, weeks and months are related and a reasonable appreciation of the meaning of terms such as an 'hour' and a 'minute'. The child will find it easier to learn to tell the time if she already knows how certain times of the day are related to regular daily events, such as getting up in the morning, having meals, watching a television programme that starts at the same time every day, and going to bed in the evening.

Things to do

- For a child who is only just beginning to understand numbers, you can introduce the following simple game: 'I'm waving one hand. Can you wave one hand? Now two hands', (waving two hands). 'Can you wave two hands? Now watch what I do and try to do the same.' (Wave one or two hands.) Larger numbers can be introduced by using several fingers.
- It is easy to invent games that will help a child to learn basic concepts of quantity and dimension. For example, when talking about size you could say: 'Here are two potatoes. One is big, the other is smaller. Let's give the big potato to teddy and the small potato to your woolly dog.'
- When helping your child to understand length, you can

say 'I've got three pieces of spaghetti [or straws, or sticks, or strips of cardboard]. Which is the longest? Which is the shortest?'.

- Introduce games in which you ask 'Which is higher?' [or wider or shorter or longer or thicker or heavier] as you show successive pairs of toys or household objects.
- Introduce numbers and counting whenever an opportunity presents itself in your daily routine. Sometimes you can do the counting, sometimes your child can do it. In some instances, you can count the objects first, and then ask the child to copy you, with or without prompts. Introduce the idea of counting into your conversations as naturally as possible:

'We need two eggs. Here they are: one, two.'

'Let's choose three books today; one, two, three.'

'How many cups have I got here? One, two. Now let's find some saucers to go with them, one for this cup and another for that cup: one, two; that's two saucers.'

- Numbers play a big part in almost any board or card game, and provide endless opportunities to count the numbers of cards, numbers of moves, numbers of counters, and so on.
- Playing shop is a useful way of learning about money, and is lots of fun for a child. Either counters or real coins can be used for money. Keep prices simple at first, introducing the idea of 'change' gradually.
- Play games which involve grouping objects and classifying them. For instance: 'Put the blue bricks in this pile and the green bricks over here.' Or 'The large marbles here, the small marbles here.' You can combine grouping and counting: 'How many blue beads? How many green beads? Now let's count them all: so, three blues plus two green ones make five altogether.'

- Try a game in which you clap your hands various numbers of times. 'Watch me, I'm clapping my hands: once, twice. Now watch me and when I've finished you clap your hands the same number of times.'
- Make use of opportunities to dramatize number concepts. Sometimes rhythm adds to the fun. Familiar examples are 'One potato, two potatoes, three potatoes, four' and 'Fly away Peter, fly away Paul'.
- Pegboards and regularly shaped objects like bricks and building blocks can be especially helpful because they clarify relationships between numbers and quantities. The child can immediately see that a line made of six bricks (or six pegs) is longer than a line of four.
- 'Disappearing' games with objects or cards can help to make a child think about things she cannot actually see and do simple sums with them. For example: 'You give me one card. Now another card. [Parent hides them.] Now how many do you think I've got? Two? Let's see if you are right. One, two. Yes, that's right.'
- Play measuring games. You can measure and compare all kinds of things: a child's own hand against yours, toy cars, soft toys. With dolls, you can progress from 'Who is the tallest?' to 'Who is the shortest?' and finish up with 'How many blocks high is teddy?'
- Weighing is an activity you can enjoy with a child, particularly when cooking. Even if a child does not understand everything you are doing, there will be good opportunities to see how measuring and counting enter into your everyday activities.
- With addition and subtraction, it is a good idea to think of lots of everyday problems, and use these opportunities for practising simple arithmetic. Try to think of activities where there is a practical purpose for knowing the answer. Here are some examples:

'Here is the post. There are three letters and two cards. How many does that make in all?'

'Let's go to the library. I have one book to take back and you have three. How many does that make?'

'Let's see how many pints of milk we have. There's one in the fridge and here are two that the milkman has just brought. So how many have we got in all?'

'We have not got many biscuits left. How many biscuits are there in the jar: one, two three. OK, I'm giving you one now, so how many are there left? Look, one, two.'

At a later stage, you can play the game while the jar is hidden from the child's sight. Then bring the jar back again for the child to check whether the answer is correct.

'There are four spoons in this drawer, but I'm taking two to eat breakfast with. How many are still in the drawer?'

- When adding and subtracting, encourage children to use their fingers for counting, invaluable assets at the stage when children can only add when they have concrete objects in mind. Counting on fingers is helpful for a young child, because fingers provide a transition between concrete objects and the abstract idea of number. Some parents worry about the possibility of a child's arithmetic skills becoming too dependent on fingers, but there is absolutely no need to be concerned about that in a preschool child.

Learning to tell the time

Most children don't learn to tell the time until relatively late, but with parental help many of them could learn it much earlier than they do. It is a useful skill for helping a child to become independent. There isn't one 'best' way to teach your child to tell the time. Progress will depend upon what she already knows. You will need a reasonably large wooden or cardboard clock face with Arabic numerals, on which the hour and minute hands can be moved separately.

Telling the time involves combining a number of skills. Children (and adults too) become confused when they have to learn a number of new things at the same time, so to avoid this, aim at dividing the learning sequence into small stages. In this way only one new skill is being taught at a time.

If your child seems to be having difficulties learning the skill you are trying to teach, ask yourself what she needs to know and understand beforehand. Quite often, the reason for a child's failure at any one stage is that she lacks some necessary prior knowledge. If you find that progress is very slow and frustrating, it may be a good idea to wait a few months to allow your child to expand her number skills and develop her conceptual understanding of time.

Here is a learning sequence that would be appropriate for a child of around five years of age who has already mastered counting and can do simple additions and subtractions. Don't rush it, don't feel that you have to follow this sequence rigidly, and make sure that learning sessions are brief and enjoyable. If your child seems bored or restless, it is time to stop. If the child gets really stuck or frustrated, abandon time-telling altogether for a while. As always, keep things light-hearted.

- Check that the child already has some understanding of periods of time such as one hour, one day, five minutes, one minute. If the concept of 'a minute' is very hazy, try playing a game in which your child has to tell you when the minute hand reaches a certain place on the clock ('Tell me when the minute hand reaches fifteen, twenty, thirty'). If you combine this game with another activity (maybe putting on a sock, or building a castle out of bricks) she will find it easier to relate the notion of time to a familiar task. That will make time a more comprehensible thing.

• Be sure that your child understands how 'a half' and 'a quarter' are related to the whole of something – use objects like fruit or biscuits to help a child to learn these concepts.

• Get the child to practise setting the hour hand on her toy clockface to various times of the day. (At this stage it is a good idea to remove the minute hand altogether, if possible.)

• Explain the meaning of 'half past' an hour, and show the appropriate position of the hour hand. Get your child to practise setting the hour hand for 'half past' various hours. Give the child lots of practice setting the hands herself and also 'reading' times that you have set.

• Once the hour hand has been mastered, you can switch attention to the minute hand. If it is convenient to do so, remove the hour hand altogether at first.

• Show how 'half past', 'quarter past', and 'quarter to' are depicted by the minute hand, and get your child to practise setting the minute hand at these positions. Now explain that an hour is divided into sixty minutes, with the quarters being at fifteen, thirty, and forty-five minutes respectively. Show that the clock face is divided up so that it takes the minute hand five minutes to move from one 'hour' position to the next. As with the hour hand, make sure that both 'reading' and 'setting' tasks are practised.

• Get your child to practise setting the minute hand at one minute past the hour, two minutes, three minutes and so on. Then show her how she can set the hand at five, ten, fifteen minutes and so on, without having to count every single minute. This may be difficult for a child who has no experience of multiplying, so be very patient. Help her to see how particular times in minutes are related to the main divisions on the clock. For example, twenty past the hour comes five minutes after quarter past.

- When the hour hand and the minute hand have both been mastered, your child can start setting both hands and begin telling the time. At first, keep to the simpler times, such as whole hours and half and quarter past the hours. Once the child can easily read times like three o'clock, half past five, quarter to eight, start on other times, such as ten past two, twenty to seven.

- Eventually a child will need to know about 24-hour clocks. You can leave that until quite a bit later, although some children will have learned about the relationship between 12- and 24-hour times from digital clocks and the video player at home.

10 | Physical Activities

From birth, babies begin the process of learning to control and use their bodies effectively. Broadly, the same *sequence* of physical development is followed by all babies and children, but each follows this sequence at his or her own individual rate, so some children of the same age can be at different stages of development. The term 'gross motor skills' refers to the large movements a child eventually learns to make, like walking, and 'fine motor skills' refers to smaller movements, usually involving the hands, like drawing and writing.

One of the first tasks babies have to learn is how to support their heads. There is a strong instinct to do this and a baby lying prone will, from day one, make an effort to lift and turn her head towards a parent's voice. By three weeks most babies are beginning to support their heads, albeit momentarily, and by six weeks will be able to raise the head slightly in order to turn it from side to side. It is not until around three months, however, that the baby will be able to lift her head right up while lying on her stomach.

A baby's developmental progress, both physically and intellectually, is an interactive process. Supporting her head enables her to look around and see more. Lying on her back and waving her arms around enables her to see her hands and begin to use them in a constructive way. Sitting up frees the arms and hands to play with objects, and opens up the field of vision still further. Crawling provides an opportunity to get hold of something currently out of reach, and walking makes this even more possible.

Stimulation and encouragement help a baby to make progress and to explore what her body can do. If nothing interesting comes into view, or her physical movement is hampered by clothing, a baby will continue to make some sort of progress yet there will be less incentive to do so. Providing the opportunities for babies to make physical progress has been demonstrated to be effective, and there is research evidence to show that doing so also brings long-term advantages to a child. Responsive parents will often instinctively create such opportunities. All the neurones, or nerve cells, exist in the brain at birth, but the system for transmitting messages in the brain is undeveloped. During the first two years of life this system develops rapidly. Also, the protective covering of the brain cells, myelin, which increases the effectiveness of the brain's transmission of messages, is incomplete at birth but virtually complete by the age of two. So there is dramatic physical and intellectual development in the first and second year of life that is dependent on the brain's development. That in turn is partly dependent on the stimulation the brain receives which helps to create the neural pathways, whose formation contributes so significantly to what we call learning.

The cortex, which amongst other things controls physical actions, is the least developed part of the brain at birth, but by the age of two it has developed enormously.

The following activities are good to try with babies up to six months and will help you explore the physical world together.

- Allow your baby to spend time moving her limbs unhindered by clothing. Make sure the room is warm and your baby is happy doing this; some babies don't like it, in which case leave it for a while and try again later. Alternatively, have your baby in the bath with you so that the feeling of water and your skin contact is reassuring (the bath water needs to be right for your baby, probably cooler than you would normally have it).

- Gently lay your baby along your lap, with her head at your knees and her feet touching and pushing against your stomach. In this position you can hold her hands, moving her arms and talking to her while she wriggles safely, stretching her legs, pushing them against your stomach and strengthening her muscles.
- Lay your baby gently on her stomach on a blanket on the floor. Get down and lie facing her, talking to her and encouraging her to look up, or from side to side, by attracting her attention with a rattle or small toy.
- Seat your baby safely in a baby-seat, or prop her up safely in order that she can see further and use her arms and hands to reach out, perhaps to a mobile hanging in front of her, or to a toy you offer her, or to feel the texture of a piece of cloth.
- Gently massage your baby: this is both stimulating and relaxing, and should be pleasurable for her. It also helps to encourage movement, and is thought to help strengthen and straighten limbs.

With all these suggestions, choose a time when your baby is in a quiet, alert phase and amenable to what you are trying to do. If your baby obviously doesn't like it, always stop; it may be that on another occasion it will be enjoyable and rewarding.

ENHANCING PHYSICAL SKILLS

As your baby grows and becomes more active, she will undoubtedly become more adventurous. While every parent is concerned for the safety of their child, you should not let this make you over-restrictive. Babies and small children need to practise new skills, experiment and learn about cause and effect. What parents can do during this time is monitor a child's activities, balancing safety considerations with freedom to explore. An accident or fright while a child is practising their new skill, whatever this might be, could damage confidence. The nature of your home will play its part here – for example, if you live in a flat or bungalow your child may not become familiar with stairs and find them difficult. Equally a child whose home does have stairs but is not allowed any access to them may never learn to use stairs safely. What a child needs is the opportunity to practise using stairs safely, within the parameters of her ability and under supervision.

Before a child starts walking she will have learned to sit, crawl and stand up. She has probably been experimenting with standing up for some time, well-supported by you or an inanimate object like a chair. The next stage is what is called 'cruising'. A baby practises her upright movement, posture and balance by moving around objects, on her feet and independent of another person. She will use furniture to hold on to as she works her way around the room, probably preferring to manage this on her own rather than have you holding one or both hands. Until she is ready to take those first unaided steps, she will most probably drop to her knees and crawl across if you encourage her to come towards you.

At this stage it is worth taking some precautions to ensure her environment is safe: stabilizing rickety furniture, or removing it from the room; moving dangerous or precious objects from accessible surfaces; never leaving hot drinks within reach; avoiding tablecloths; not leaving a 'cruising' child unattended. While she is practising her walking leave her feet free of shoes, as babies glean much information from the contact their bare feet have with the floor.

For children to maximize their physical potential, they need a combination of basic ability, confidence and opportunity. Opportunities are very often dependent on parents organizing them, and may also be linked to parents' own interests. Allowing plenty of time to climb and explore, practising balancing, kicking, throwing and catching a ball, swimming, riding a bike, and so on, are important, as is making sure a child is not hampered by restrictive clothing. Some children will naturally enjoy physical activities with very little encouragement. But others will depend upon the help of an attentive and patient parent to become confident and coordinated in their movements.

Physical play, in public playgrounds, swimming pools, gyms and so on, is often a very sociable thing, and will contribute a great deal to your child's ability to mix with others.

FINE MOTOR SKILLS

Right from the beginning, you can do much to help your child acquire fine motor skills, by being aware of activities that help to practise hand-eye coordination and encourage precise muscle control. During the first twelve months a baby will spend a lot of time exploring what her hands can do, extending her skills in grabbing, swiping, holding, moving things from one hand to another and learning to release and drop objects. From a year onwards she will be starting to use her gripping abilities purposefully to feed herself, and will persistently be learning how to manipulate objects more efficiently. As usual, take your cues from the baby: follow what is fun for her and introduce new play ideas or new objects to explore and touch when you feel they would be interesting for her.

All the following activities are good practice for developing hand–eye coordination throughout the preschool year:

- self-feeding, finger foods first, eventually with a spoon, then knife and fork
- building blocks
- threading buttons
- sorting shapes and sizes
- unscrewing jar lids and bottle tops
- undoing and doing up buttons, zippers and poppers
- simple jigsaws
- using stickle bricks, duplo bricks and then lego
- drawing and painting; copying simple shapes
- using scissors

Adeptness with such skills will be very useful preparation for learning to write. Time spent in scribbling and drawing are especially significant here in helping a child to develop the control needed to form precise letter shapes with a pencil.

It is always good to encourage a baby or child to practise newly acquired skills and provide a range of opportunities to do so. It is also important to think ahead, and be prepared for the next stage. Cultural emphases differ, and this can influence expectations. For example, in the UK we don't really expect children to eat skilfully with a knife and fork until they are about five years old, whereas in China the average age at which children eat with chopsticks is two and a half. This is simply because they are expected to use chopsticks, and consequently given the encouragement and practice to do so.

THE LONG-TERM CONSEQUENCES OF EARLY MOTOR LEARNING

Early opportunities to learn physical skills do make a difference. In an investigation varying levels of early training were given to two male twins. One twin received instruction in a number of physical skills between the ages of seven and twenty-four months, on five days each week. The other twin was given less than three months' training, and it was delayed until he was twenty-two months old. The differing regimes led to large and permanent differences in levels of performance. The twin who received intensive training made faster progress, performing well above the average for boys of his age. He swam at ten months and could dive from a diving-board at seventeen months. At six years of age he was still well ahead of his brother at running, climbing, jumping, swimming and riding a bicycle, and even at the age of twenty-two years the first twin was still superior at some skills.

In other studies nursery school children who were trained over an eight-week period in skills such as kicking, long jumping, bouncing a ball and balancing on a board, achieved real gains compared with children who received no special training, and four-year-olds who were given three thirty-minute training sessions in gymnastic skills each week, over a fifteen-week period, made much bigger advances over that period.

HELPING YOUR CHILD

Getting an early start in gaining physical skills may increase a child's chances of becoming an expert player at, say, tennis or football, and there have been newspaper reports of young sports champions whose parents attribute their success to instruction that began early in childhood. Andre Agassi was receiving instruction from Bjorn Borg at the age of eight, for example. But there is no firm evidence that concentrated training in the early childhood years always has positive long-term effects, and for most parents, the dangers of intensive early training in physical skills will outweigh the possible benefits. Rather than giving a child formal instruction, it is more sensible to look for ways to make sure that everyday life provides plenty of opportunities for a child to practise making controlled and coordinated movements. Such opportunities are not hard to find: there are ball games suitable for childen of all ages, and parents who are reasonably patient and inventive find that the majority of games can be adapted to make them enjoyable for a young child.

Like most other games, those that involve physical skills teach the young learner in more ways than one. For instance, a child's social skills may benefit from experiences of having to cooperate and also compete with others, and take turns. Active play of any kind is rarely 'just' play.

If you are the kind of person who enjoys physical games and find that playing ball games with your children is a way of spending time together that seems natural and relaxing, it may be reassuring to discover that for your child this kind of activity can be valuable as well as enjoyable. It is one more example of the general principle that when parent and child are enjoying some activity together, the chances are that there will be good learning experiences for the child. However, if you dislike physical games, you should make a conscious effort to remember that physical games do play a useful role in early learning. Quite apart from the learning benefits of physical activities, exercise is essential for physical fitness, lack of exercise being a major cause of premature death in the developed world.

Almost any physical game or activity will help a child to develop useful physical skills. Running, walking, skipping, balancing, climbing, ball games, swimming, dancing, gymnastics and horseriding all provide beneficial exercise and make a child stronger, and each aids balance, control, coordination and flexibility. So far as a child's general physical coordination is concerned there is no strong reason for favouring any one of these activities over the others: don't be afraid to follow the preferences of you and your child. Studies of young athletes have shown that in most cases their parents were keen on fitness and encouraged them to enjoy physical activities from an early age.

Although sports and physical games are particularly rich in opportunities for children to practise the kinds of learning that involve making skilled movements, other daily experiences also play a part. The mundane task of learning to get dressed unaided is a major challenge and also a spur to progress. Being able to do this, and other everyday skills such as washing, eating with a knife and fork, learning to tie shoelaces, and using scissors and simple tools, are important for any child. These skills help children to become increasingly independent as they gain better control over their physical movements.

11 | Beginning School

Even if your child has enjoyed playgroup or nursery, going to school is a big adjustment and means that she has to deal with many new challenges. How can you best prepare your child for school and help her benefit fully from the time she spends there?

You can be sure that if your child has had access to some of the language and prereading experiences described in earlier chapters, she will be far better prepared for schooling than many young children are. She will have a good mastery of language and have made a start on many of the skills that reading, writing and arithmetic draw upon. Your child will be ready for classroom learning, and be prepared to make the most of all school has to offer.

Also, bear in mind that while school will present your child with unfamiliar tasks, there will be plenty of opportunities to learn how to meet new challenges. Parents don't need to anticipate each and every demand their child will meet at school: a more realistic aim is to make sure that she is well enough prepared to avoid being overwhelmed by whatever is new or unfamiliar.

Starting full-time school is a time of transition for all small children and, to some extent, their parents. From now on another significant influence will be affecting your child as she moves away from the family into the wider world, becoming increasingly independent. How your child begins to cope with daily life at school will depend on several things: how much preparation a child has had at meeting the world outside the immediate family; whether she is socially confident, very shy or somewhere in between; and how *you* feel about your child starting school.

Your feelings may be influenced by your own memories of early schooldays. If you loved school as a child, you will probably anticipate that your child will too. If you were a reluctant pupil you may well view the beginning of your child's formal education with unnecessary trepidation on her behalf. Either way, it is worth remembering that your child's experience of starting school will be very different from yours. It is also important to respect a child's own view of school, rather than imposing your own, listening to what she has to say about this new experience and allowing her to formulate her own views.

How do *parents* experience the first days of school? Here are some reactions to the question 'What effect did your child's starting school have on you as a parent?':

'I had been looking forward to him going. He was ready to and so was I! It was good to have some time apart. The term before he was due to go he was wild, he was ready for more than the playgroup could offer.'

'I found I missed him terribly.'

'It was a wrench to be separated after four and a half years of teaching him virtually everything he knew and a feeling that I was losing him to an outside influence over which I would have no control.'

'Jane had been looking forward to it, but for me it was a new lease of life. I felt it was time to be myself again and find a little job.'

'I felt I took a back seat, as he enjoyed going to school and was full of what he had been doing. I also felt that he didn't need me quite as much, so only having John I was a bit alone with my thoughts, but pleased he was happy about school.'

'A sense of excitement and of loss, earlier mornings! His younger sister became more talkative.'

FINDING AND CHOOSING A SCHOOL

In theory, in the UK you are entitled to send your child to the school of your choice, although in practice this may not be possible if the school is oversubscribed. When that happens, the school defines its own admission policy, usually based on considerations such as the distance a child lives from a school and whether a child has a brother or sister already in the school. Local Education Authorities have a legal obligation to publish their schools' admissions policies, so this information is easily obtained.

A question of choice will arise only if there are a selection of schools to choose from. If you live in the middle of a rural area there may be only one school available. If there is a choice, it is undoubtedly worth taking the time to visit any schools you may be considering, making a preliminary decision and getting your child's application recorded. Nearer the time of school entry, you will be informed as to whether or not your child has a place. If any problems arise about admission you should contact your Local Education Authority which will advise you.

Always weigh up the practicalities of a particular school. For instance, if it is going to take you forty-five anxious minutes of rush-hour travelling to get there, is it really worth it? Also, if a child attends school some distance from the area in which he or she lives, mixing with playmates and building up friendships after school or during holidays can be a problem.

In Britain education becomes compulsory in the term after a child's fifth birthday, although most areas admit children either in the term, or the academic year, that they are five, when they are described as 'rising fives'. For a child born in the summer, this could mean starting in the reception class of a primary school quite soon after the fourth birthday. In the same class there may be children who are already five, as their fifth birthday was in the September of that academic year. So the age range in a reception class may be almost as much as a year, and with four and five year olds this can make a real difference in ability and maturity. It is one reason why reception class teachers place as much emphasis on learning to cope with school as on academic accomplishments.

It is not necessarily advantageous for a child to start school the minute she is offered a place. If your child has not reached the age at which starting school is compulsory and does not seem ready for it, don't feel pressurized to take up the place then. You have the right to refuse and defer the starting date until the term after your child's fifth birthday. Your decision on this may be determined by the style of reception class she will be entering. If the class is very formal, with lots of time spent sitting still at a desk and little scope for free expression, then your four year old might be happier remaining at home or in some sort of preschool group. It is so important that your child's first experience of school is positive, and if the early stages are over-demanding it could influence how school is perceived for a long time. A child cannot learn adequately unless he or she is relaxed and confident.

Most schools expect and encourage parents to visit the school in advance, to see it in action, either singly or in prearranged groups. Arrangements to visit can be made through the headteacher or the school secretary; it is well worth doing, and gives you an opportunity to find out how the school works. One fairly typical prospective parent told us:

After having a chat with the headteacher, who took down our child's details on the application form, we were shown round the school by two pupils from the top class. It was quite touching to see their obvious pride in their school, and they were very informative about all sorts of things that children notice but that another adult probably wouldn't think to point out. We also sat in on an assembly during which two of the oldest boys had a scrap. The confidence with which the staff dealt with this was impressive and, overall, contributed to a very positive view of the school.

Once a school place has been confirmed, usually towards the end of the preceding academic year, you can begin to talk to your child about that particular school. Initially this will probably be only in passing – you might point it out when you pass, or mention that the little boy down the road already goes there.

In many schools, reception classes welcome children into the classroom for regular visits before they start, for stories and games. It is undoubtedly a good idea to take advantage of these opportunities if possible. They give parent and child a chance to look around and get used to the school, and become familiar with the larger areas such as the hall and dining area, and also the toilets. It is equally important for parent and child to talk about school during the months before it begins, so the child is able to express any anxieties, and for you to provide much needed advice and reassurance, and prepare her for the practical necessities of everyday life at school.

SOCIAL DEVELOPMENT AND THE SCHOOL CHILD

Settling into an unfamiliar environment will not be a totally new experience for a child who is already accustomed to spending time in a nursery school or kindergarten. Even so, for most children, their first 'proper' school may seem larger and rather impersonal, demanding bigger adjustments and more conformity than has previously been necessary.

As well as the practical skills necessary at school, a child will need to aquire various social skills in order to get on with adults and other children. It is quite possible for a young child to be adequately prepared to handle classroom learning tasks, yet totally unprepared for the social relationships which form a large part of classroom life. A child who has spent little time with people outside the family may not know how to deal with the social demands of daily life in the school community.

Most children who have attended a nursery school or preschool playgroup will have had good opportunities to learn how to socialize. But the availability of preschool opportunities is highly variable in Britain: 95% of children receive some form of nursery education in Manchester, for example, whereas in Devon only 11% do so. The Rumbold report of 1990 highlighted the discrepancy in nationwide provision, the result of which is that in some areas children are much more prepared for learning outside the home than others.

With or without formal preschool provision, there is much that parents can do to provide social opportunities outside the immediate family. Although parents are naturally wary about encouraging their children to talk to strangers, there are lots of 'non-strangers' who may be familiar to your family – in local shops, on public transport, at the library – with whom a child can learn to develop the confidence needed to communicate successfully. When someone addresses a question or comment to your child, encourage her to listen and answer, rather than answering for her. Remind her of recent experiences that she can use conversationally, for example, 'Tell Mr Jones what you had for your birthday'. What may start as monosyllabic answers will, with practice, improve as your child's confidence and vocabulary grows. The habit of talking loudly and clearly enough to be heard, and listening attentively to any response, both of which are practised in these situations, are invaluable in the classroom.

Children attending school, or preschool, have to learn to be part of a group. When it comes to settling into school, being socially competent is more important than knowing about letters and numbers. A child learns to share and take turns in group situations, where an adult is there to give guidance. A certain amount of this gets learned quite naturally in families where there are several children, but with a first or only child it is less easy to provide this experience at home, and you may have to work at it. Take the time to meet regularly with friends who also have children, visit the library for storytelling sessions, or participate in a preschool playgroup, even if this may mean a bit of a hike.

Children arriving at school without at least some social and practical skills will spend a large part of their early days learning those things. One primary school headteacher says, 'If they don't settle in easily, it delays their academic progress. They may catch up but it could take a long time'. The reception class teacher at the same school finds that the children arrive at very different stages both academically and socially: some can read, others can barely make themselves understood; one lies on the floor and refuses to do as he is told; another is spoilt at home, and refuses to tidy up; another is a loner whom his classmates taunt. Some of the children in this reception class have been to either a playgroup or a private nursery, and they are noticeably more confident, able to mix more easily with their peers. It can take a couple of terms at least for some children to settle well enough to begin 'learning', as we would identify it.

PRACTICAL CONCERNS

By no means all the concerns which parents and children express in connection with starting school are about learning and education. Practical day to day issues loom larger. There are worries about being separated from the parent and having to share the teacher's attention with a large number of children, anxieties about changing for PE and using the toilet, and concerns about dealing with lunchtime routines and coping at playtime with large numbers of bigger children. There are numerous ways in which parents can help their child, although it isn't possible to anticipate everything (which is why listening to what a child has to say is so important).

Many of the practical problems arise simply because schools have to teach large numbers of children. So it helps a great deal if a child is able to get dressed reasonably quickly, wash without making a mess, and, when applicable, tie shoelaces efficiently. Although you may have conscientiously taught your child practical skills such as using a knife and fork, doing up shoes, putting on and fastening a coat, visiting the lavatory alone and washing hands, the chances are that the child will have done them only in response to your request. At school children are expected to get on with things without endless cajoling or help.

You will need to use your imagination and anticipate what may prove difficult for a child. For example, the zip fastener on Jane's coat is slightly stiff, and her mother has got into the habit of always adjusting the coat for her. At home, that saves time and is convenient for everyone, but as soon as Jane starts school, without an adult to help her, she may be in difficulties. She is not helped by the fact that dealing with an awkward zip is even harder when there are lots of other noisy children around. And if her problems with her coat are compounded by difficulties with other practical tasks, such as changing shoes, it is easy to see that these problems could loom large in her school day.

In adult eyes, problems like these can seem trivial, but for an anxious child they can be baffling. For young children there is nothing more stressful than to be placed with no advance warning in a situation for which they are unprepared and unskilled.

Visiting the lavatory alone causes anxiety for many children. Although they are able to manage perfectly well at home, school lavatories are a different matter altogether. They can be cold and unfriendly places, and a child has to ask if she can go. There is no one to remind her that she may want to go, and verify that she gets there in time.

Here are the comments of a teacher on some of the daily realities of classroom life:

I have found that there are quite a few problems which are relatively easily overcome. The tying of shoelaces is a continuing bind for teachers everywhere, not just tying and untying them for PE but in the playground when they become undone. Velcro fastenings for the youngest children do help to make the child more independent and are a teacher's best friend! When parents are buying a winter coat, do they check the fastenings? Is there a possibility of the child being able to fasten the coat, is the zip fiddly or strong and easy to grip? Dungarees are often too time-consuming to unfasten for young children and can lead to toilet accidents, whereas track-suit top and simple trousers allow the child to dress quickly. Children should practise all aspects of putting clothes on and off, before starting school if possible, and during the early stages. Once your preschool child has tried on the uniform ask him or her to change from that into a gym kit. It helps if the parent encourages children to fold clothes neatly and tidily – imagine a class of thirty leaving socks and shirts all over the floor! It tends to cause anxiety in the child and anger in the parent if things go missing or get lost. Of course, putting the child's name on all items of clothing is helpful, especially if the child can recognize his or her own name. To help, parents could mark names with a colour-permanent felt marker, so that the child need not rely just on reading but on colour recognition too.

FIRST DAYS AT SCHOOL

With children, it is wise to take nothing for granted. One little boy, talking with his mother about school – at this stage a completely unknown quantity – listened attentively to everything she was saying, and then asked, 'Do they have toilets at school?'. Another child, having spent a happy first day at school was surprised and even dismayed to discover that she was expected to go back again the next day, and the next. 'But I've been to school,' was her plaintive cry. Unless the purpose of school is made clear to children well in advance, basic misunderstandings such as these can easily arise. Parents need to consider the limitations of a four or five year old's experience, especially if there are no older siblings who already go to school. Parents also need to be aware of the limitations of having a vocabulary of only around 2,000 words. Unless you explain new vocabulary to her before she starts school, a child will not understand some of the words she will meet there. Words like lesson, dinner-lady, assembly, headteacher, playtime, playground, don't make much sense until you have been to school.

In *Cider with Rosie* the writer Laurie Lee tells this story of his first day at school:

I spent the first day picking holes in paper and then went home in a smouldering temper.

'What's the matter love, didn't you like it at school then?'

'They never gave me a present.'

'Present, what present?'

'They said they'd give me a present.'

'Well now I'm sure they didn't.'

'They did, they said: "You're Laurie Lee, aren't you? Well you just sit there for the present." I sat there all day but I never got it. I ain't going back there again.'

Recent research conducted by Gillian Barrett at the Centre for Applied Research in Education pinpointed many aspects of starting school which children find difficult. Not surprisingly she discovered that many children did not know what to do, and felt there was 'too much of everything'. Children also found that not being able to do things like drawing and writing when they felt like it, and sitting on the floor cross-legged, upset them, and many didn't like school dinners. They also found the older children too rough, the school and its playground too big and noisy, and the lunch playtime too long. Although the majority adapt to what is required of them at school, their ability to do so will undoubtedly be influenced by how confident they feel.

Gillian Barrett's research also drew attention to how tiring small children found their school day. For six long hours they were expected to be part of a large group, even larger at playtimes, and to conform to a particular standard of behaviour. Most children manage this admirably, but they may be exhausted, and irritable, and prone to demonstrating this in no uncertain terms the moment you collect them from school. In that first term, bear these things in mind, and don't expect too much from your child. If your child's behaviour at home seems to have deteriorated, it doesn't necessarily mean that there is an enormous problem at school: perhaps she is just letting go rather dramatically when the school day is finished. For many children an immediate drink, something to eat and time to recuperate help a lot. It took one mother a whole term to realize that her daughter never took a drink at school because at home the water was always filtered and from a jug and she wasn't sure she should drink from the fountain or take what was offered at lunchtime. Six hours is too long for a child to go without a drink, and both parent and teacher had to pay attention to this problem. Having too many after-school activities in the first term can add to your child's difficulties, as she may become more and more overtired.

Teachers are keen to do what they can to help children settle and parents relax, and will be happy to give an outline of the school week, so that you know when PE and other regular activities take place, and are better prepared to talk to your child about the school day. Some schools make monthly menus available, so that parents can see what food is on offer. Sometimes it is even possible for a parent to sit in on lunch at school with a child who has just started.

On the very first day, or week, of school many children often attend only half-time. Many teachers find that throughout the earliest months of school a full day at school is too long for some children, and some schools have a half day attendance for new children for perhaps half a term. Reception class staff would often prefer a child to be taken home after lunch rather than having an overtired youngster clinging to the teacher throughout the afternoon.

LEARNING AT SCHOOL

Many of the activities described in the previous chapters will help a child to be ready for school, but there are a number of other things that parents can do. Here we look at some ways to make your child better prepared for aspects of school learning which, simply because of their unfamiliarity, can cause problems.

Ideally, child, parent and teacher would work together as a close team. In reality the amount of consultation between teacher and parent can be very limited, and although there are many schools that genuinely encourage regular meetings and discussion there are others in which the number of parent-teacher contacts averages no more than three or four per year. Parents are understandably anxious not to be seen by teachers as 'pushy', yet it is worth making a serious effort to get to know your child's teacher.

Schools vary enormously in the extent to which parents are encouraged to contribute. In the early years, most schools welcome parents who are willing to help in the classroom. If it is practically possible, try to participate in this way; you will learn a great deal about the daily events in your child's life from the experience, as well as finding out about the curriculum.

School learning is more deliberate than that which you have shared at home. It is likely to be less immediately useful or obviously 'natural'. To say this is not to criticize school learning, since education is designed to prepare people to live in modern societies, and these, by the standards of people living in the past, are indeed artificial and unnatural. So school learning needs to be different from the more natural kinds of everyday learning that takes place at home. It has to be in order to achieve its aims.

Try putting yourself in the position of a child going to school for the first time. Here are some of the ways in which you might find that learning at school is different from anything you have experienced at home. You may remember experiencing some of these problems when you first began school.

1 At school, there are few adults to help you when you need assistance, because there are so many other children. You cannot count on an immediate response to your questions or requests for advice. Instead of having plenty of adult attention, you have to share one adult with a number of other children.

2 Instead of being able to depend upon the presence of familiar parents whom you have known as long as you can remember, you have to deal with a relative stranger who is struggling to get acquainted with all the children in the classroom and may have only a vague knowledge of what you yourself can and cannot do.

3 Perhaps for the first time you are being asked to learn and remember things for their own sake. At school, unlike home, there is not always an immediate or practical reason for the learning activities you are asked to do. That is not to say that there won't be a reason, but that may not be at all clear. A teacher may start a new topic just by saying, 'Today we are all going to learn about . . .' without indicating why. For some children, the teacher who first says 'I want you to remember . . .' may be giving them a task that is quite unfamiliar. And many youngsters will know very little about the kinds of things you can do in order to help remember something. A few children will begin school with only the haziest notion of what it means to 'remember'.

4 At school you are required to concentrate on what your teacher says, and at the same time ignore all the distractions caused by noisy children in the classroom. At home, your parents usually know when you mishear what they say or fail to understand. They are usually happy to repeat themselves when they see the need. This is less likely to happen at school.

5 At home you can do most things at your own pace. At school you may have to adjust the timing of your actions to the wishes of the teacher and the pace set by other children. At home, when you get tired or bored with one activity you can do something else. At school this may not be possible.

6 Some of the activities that you are expected to engage in at school may be entirely unfamiliar. You may find them very difficult, or you may see no point in doing them, and you may not be at all sure what exactly it is that you are expected to be doing. You can find yourself thoroughly confused and doing everything incorrectly. The help you require may not be forthcoming, because the teacher cannot assist a large number of children all at the same time.

7 Sometimes, to add to the frustration you experience when you find that tasks are confusing or difficult, you discover that other children are making much better progress than you. Perhaps, for example, others find it easier to identify words or write letters. You may think that they are doing better than you, and feel upset about this.

Reception class teachers make a big effort to ease children into the new learning environment of school, and are fully aware that children are often unequally prepared for the kinds of learning tasks they meet at school. There is a limit, however, to what is humanly possible within the constraints of an average school classroom – which is why your efforts to give appropriate preparation are so vital.

'Appropriate' is a key word here. The culture of a school happens to be one in which those kinds of learning that are based on language and symbols, on written and numerical forms of communication, are valued and stressed. Other kinds of learning, including some that are very important outside school, get less emphasis. So it is a child who has good language skills, some knowledge of letters and words and a degree of basic competence with numbers who will be ready for the learning experiences to be encountered in the classroom.

At school, it is often very useful for a child to possess 'how to learn' skills that will improve her chances of acquiring and remembering new information. These include useful mental strategies such as rehearsing, self-testing, discovering ways of categorizing new information and connecting it to what she already knows.

A familiar way in which adults and children gain control over new information is by rehearsing. Simply by repeating information that we have just read or heard, we can increase the likelihood of keeping it in memory. Throughout our lives, rehearsal provides a valuable aid to remembering; it is simple, convenient, and can be used many times every day.

Children who are able to rehearse and do so regularly have a big advantage over those who do not. It is easy to tell when children are rehearsing, as they usually move their lips. In one research study, children of different ages looked at pictures of objects they had been told to try to remember. It turned out that most of the ten year olds did rehearse, but among the five year olds only one child in ten did. In both age groups those children who did rehearse recalled more items than those who did not – so it is likely that rehearsing led to better memorizing.

What happens when you teach rehearsing to children who do not already do so? Does it improve their remembering? If it does, might it be a good idea to teach all young children how to rehearse? To answer these questions, the researchers selected some of the children in the study who did not rehearse, and carefully taught them how to. That turned out to be easy; the children were simply told to whisper the names of the objects they were looking at, and they quickly got the hang of that. It soon became clear that rehearsing considerably increased their ability to memorize, which now equalled that of the children who had rehearsed spontaneously.

So teaching non-rehearsers to rehearse is definitely a good idea. If your child has not already discovered for himself how to, there is much to be gained from teaching her to apply this simple learning strategy. In a typical school day there will be plenty of occasions when quietly rehearsing some information will improve a child's performance. All you have to do to start a child rehearsing is to encourage him to whisper to himself the information he is keen to remember. The Things to Do section that follows describes some games that help achieve this.

In practice, some extra encouragement will be needed, because for a child to get into the habit of rehearsing it is necessary not just to know how to rehearse but also for the activity to become a habit. Otherwise, despite the fact that it is useful, the child may forget to rehearse. Different learning tasks call for different amounts of rehearsal and subtly different rehearsing strategies. But you will not need to teach your child about this. Once she gains the habit of rehearsing she will discover how to adapt the skill to various situations.

There are other ways in which school-age children can exercise more control over their learning activities, although none of the other strategies are quite as powerful or as easy to apply. Children will often develop such strategies independently, or follow suggestions from their teachers. They can help themselves to remember by mentally grouping or categorizing items of information. They may find it helpful to develop ways of visualizing things in order to memorize them. Mnemonics (meaning memory aids) are another way of remembering unfamiliar terms or ideas – children enjoy making up their own versions.

An effective teacher will often find ways of making a learning task easier by connecting something that is entirely unfamiliar to the child to something she already knows. In everyday life we make such links all the time – for example, whenever we use metaphors to aid communication, we are doing just that.

Apart from rehearsing skills, parents should not feel it necessary to teach their preschool child the more sophisticated learning strategies, but it is a good idea to play some memory games. They give valuable practice at careful concentration and encourage a child to make an active effort to remember.

TALKING TO YOUR CHILD ABOUT SCHOOL

Parents are sometimes slow to learn that asking a child what their day was like is a notoriously unsuccessful way to elicit information. Even asking quite specific things like 'What did you have for lunch?' or 'Who did you sit next to in class?' is prone to yield the response 'I can't remember'. The questions a parent asks after the end of the school day are particularly likely to get this kind of response. Don't think that your child is deliberately excluding you or rejecting you. Children live very much in the present, and what they had for lunch is largely irrelevant three hours after the event. You may well find that information will be more forthcoming later, during a quiet time after your child has come home and relaxed for a while. It is worth getting into the habit of talking through your children's day with them as they volunteer information, acquainting yourself with what is important in their life, sharing the good times and providing support during the bad. Tell them about your own day. Primary school life can be quite emotionally intense for many children, and your sympathy is tremendously important.

Conversations about school will be easier if you familiarize yourself with the life of the school, the people there and the things that are happening. Most primary schools welcome parental support, which can be given in a variety of ways, and many schools encourage parents to come into the classroom to help, perhaps hearing children read. Class outings invariably require parent helpers. Helping out like this means you will get to know the other children which certainly makes conversations with yours flow more easily. You will undoubtedly hear a lot about the class teacher, who for many small children becomes something of a guru.

You cannot share every minute of your child's day at school, and even if you tried to do so you would risk interfering with her growing independence. But there is much that you can do to help a child to make the most of school. Your being available to listen, your interest and encouragment all contribute to a child's self-esteem.

Sharing your own childhood experiences of school – putting up with a difficult classmate, the agonies of school lunches, winning a race – will make it easier for your children to deal with their problems and open up real conversations. In any event if, after a day at school, they come home knowing that you, at least, will be on their side and will give them a fair hearing, they will be able to cope more confidently with the school day. Children learn far better at school when they are confident and free from anxieties.

WHEN PROBLEMS OCCUR

You won't always see eye to eye with your child's teacher, but it is easier to resolve disagreements if people are sufficiently relaxed with one another to feel that matters of concern can be raised in a frank and open manner.

The job of being an effective classroom teacher is a difficult one, and although you will probably have a lot of respect for the majority of your child's teachers, it is possible that at some stage you will be genuinely unhappy about the way in which a particular teacher seems to be behaving towards your child. Carol Baker, the author of *Helping Your Schoolchild* (Longman, 1991) has some good advice about what to do when things seem to be going wrong. First, she says, talk to the teacher, being careful not to do this in an accusing way but describing the problem as clearly and objectively as you can. So far you have only your child's account of the situation to go on, and children's perceptions can be very one-sided, particularly when there is any kind of personality clash between teacher and child.

Also, bear in mind that your child is one of many for whom the teacher is responsible and that actions which to your child appear 'unfair' or unreasonable may be a teacher's best efforts to meet the diverse needs and interests of a large number of very different children.

When you are talking to the teacher, try to avoid criticizing him or her as a person, and confine your remarks to the particular problems that are concerning you. Rather than blatantly saying 'My son complains that your lessons are boring,' it is much better to appear less obviously critical. You might say, for example, 'I haven't seen much written work by Mark this term. Are you happy about his writing?' This gives you a tactful way into the discussion. Carol Baker recommends being careful not to say anything to a teacher that would make you feel defensive if it was said to you. Make a point of commenting on aspects of her teaching that you appreciate. Like other people, teachers don't like to lose face, so don't expect an immediate promise or apology as soon as you have pointed out that a problem exists. The chances are that the teacher will have taken note of your comments, all the same.

If your approaches to the teacher do not produce a satisfactory outcome, you may feel that there is no alternative but to speak to the headteacher. Don't do this until you have at least tried talking to your child's classroom teacher. If you do see the head, remember to keep to the facts and resist any temptation to indulge in personal criticism of the teacher's character. Just say what is going wrong.

Most headteachers will do what they can, but their scope for action is not unlimited. Schools have to work with the staff they have, however imperfect. So while it may be true that your child would be happier to move from Mrs Y's class to Mrs X's, if a lot of parents feel the same way there may be no way in which the headteacher can meet your wishes without inviting further problems. In most cases some kind of positive action will be possible, but be aware that your preferred solution may not be one that is desirable from the school's viewpoint.

Perhaps inevitably, this chapter has emphasized ways of avoiding problems that can arise at school. For most children, however, most of the time school is a positive experience, offering rich opportunities to learn, to grow and to make friends.

Things to do

Many activities which prepare a child for school are described in previous chapters. Here we include just a few additional suggestions to those that will help your child adjust to the particular demands of the school classroom.

In the classroom it is often important to be able to listen carefully to the teacher's voice. The following listening games will provide useful practice.

- Whispering. Parent and child have conversations in which they talk more and more quietly, to see how accurately each can hear what the other is saying.
- Try combining whispering with a 'Sarah says, do this' game, in which one partner gives the instructions, and the other obeys. Parent and child should take turns to give and receive instructions.
- Alternatively, play a 'Sarah says . . .' game with the radio

turned on quite loud. This is another way of giving your child practice in listening carefully under different hearing conditions.

Memory games

- Playing 'pairs' is a good way of sharpening the memory – you can play it with any cards used for 'Snap'. Try to make sure that you keep the number of cards small enough to ensure that your child will be correct on a reasonably large number of occasions.
- Play 'Kim's game'. You simply put a number of familiar objects on a board, and tell your child that she will have, say, one minute to inspect the objects. Afterwards you cover the board and ask the child to tell you the objects she can remember.
- The task can be made harder or easier by varying the number of objects, or the inspection time, or both. Claims that playing this game 'improves memory' are not entirely realistic, but it does help children to learn that they can remember things better when they concentrate and make a real effort to remember, and it gives them opportunities to practise doing so.

Rehearsing

- To teach your child to rehearse, ask her to whisper more and more quietly, until she cannot actually hear what she is saying. Then ask the child to try doing this with a list of ten words that you say aloud, at a rate of one per second. Explain that rehearsing is a way of 'keeping in your head' new information, in order to improve remembering.
- Vary the circumstances in which your child rehearses. For example, try asking her to rehearse when she is

looking at pictures of objects rather than listening. When this is mastered, experiment by having her rehearse items in groups rather than one at a time.

- Remember that in order for a child to get into the habit of rehearsing regularly, whenever there is an occasion when it would be helpful, it is not enough just to have learned *how* to rehearse. The child also needs to have practised rehearsing often enough for it to have become a *habit*, and to some extent automatic. To reach that state of affairs it is necessary to have had plenty of opportunities to practise rehearsing.

12 | Television

Television is a good servant but a bad master, and there are few homes in which parents' worries about their children's viewing have never led to arguments. Yet it is all too easy to make television a convenient scapegoat – in fact it can, and does, enrich us all.

When people focus on the negative aspects of television they sometimes forget that children do gain valuable knowledge from what they view, even if a programme is not obviously 'educational'. And television enables children to relax at times when they need to.

How much television is too much? This is a matter of opinion. Parents have varying views about what is acceptable, and no one way of dealing with this issue is right for every family. On average, research indicates that British children of all ages watch television for around three hours a day. Nine year olds watch the most; preschoolers watch less than children at primary school, and adolescents watch the least. On the face of it these figures look alarming, but it should be borne in mind that children do watch less than adults. One study found that during a three-hour period when the television set was on, three to four year olds were only looking at the screen, on average, for sixty-five minutes. So the fear that children are totally ensnared by the medium is not entirely justified.

Young people who watch a great deal of television tend to be relatively passive children who lack confidence, do poorly in school, read little, and have few other interests. But watching large amounts of television is rarely the actual *cause* of such problems; the chances are that watching television a lot is a *symptom* of other problems rather than the reason for them. When things are going wrong for a child, turning to television can be a solace or an escape, a way of avoiding problems. If a young person has few interests or lacks friends, television is something to fall back on. There is a danger that parents who impose rigid limits on viewing because they think too much time is spent watching television are merely attacking the symptoms of a child's difficulties whilst the real causes still remain.

COPING WITH TELEVISION

Some parents try to restrict viewing times or limit the hours of viewing allowed, or attempt to specify which programmes a child is allowed to watch. Unfortunately, viewing rules and restrictions are often resented and are hard to enforce, especially when there are older brothers and sisters at home. In practice, a parent who makes an effort to enforce firm rules is likely to face a lot of opposition. Children are often skilled at emotional blackmail, and you can count on your son or daughter having a best friend whose mother permits her children to see all the programmes you would most like your child to miss. In many cases, trying to impose very strict restrictions on watching television is unrealistic. This particular battleground is sometimes best avoided.

There are some compelling reasons for taking a reasonably liberal approach to children's viewing. The first is that in the right circumstances television is an excellent source of information and ideas, and a superb window onto the wider world. Depriving a child of opportunities to watch television may limit her awareness. Consider the experience of some parents who were worried about the problems that television can create for children, and decided not to own a television set. They were forced to reconsider their decision when their son's teacher told them that the child was displaying a worrying lack of general information and knowledge of current affairs. 'Is it possible', the teacher asked, 'that Jeremy does not watch television at home?'

The teacher's concern was genuine, although it is possible that the major problem for Jeremy was not an absence of knowledge but a lack of shared experiences and information which he could talk about with his classmates. All young people have to learn how to get on with others. Shared interests, humour, likes and dislikes help to make this possible. For young people, television is a valuable source of shared knowledge that provides the basis for social contact.

Because Jeremy never watched television he did not have this important point of contact with other young people: he did not share some of the daily experiences they took for granted, and would have found it hard to participate in class discussions. He may even have found it more difficult to make friends.

LEARNING FROM TELEVISION

Television can be an excellent teacher and a rich source of knowledge. Naturally enough, parents like to see their children watching programmes that have a definite educational flavour, and many are less happy when a child prefers something that is far from educational. But when children are asked what they get out of watching television, it seems that the programmes from which they learn most are often those which, to a parent, can seem 'unsuitable'.

For instance, the kind of soap opera that many a parent would rather their ten year old avoided may be filled with information about matters which are all-important to a child of that age, but ignored in school. How do you deal with your feelings? How do you cope when you are afraid? How can you get on better with others? How do you participate in a group of people? How do you safely approach strangers or react to them? How can you make new friends? How do you control your own anger, and how should you react to nasty or bad-tempered behaviour in others? What rules are people expected to follow in the world outside home and school? How do adults differ? In what ways are other children's parents different from your own, and why? How do you cope with adults who are totally unlike the people you are used to? How do you handle yourself in situations that you have not encountered at home or at school?

When we try to see things from this perspective, it is easy to appreciate that there are powerful reasons why such knowledge is vital to a young person. You may be absolutely right when you say that the soap opera to which your child seems to be addicted is badly written, the acting is poor, and that some of the values it promotes are highly questionable. All the same, from your child's point of view, if the programme depicts characters with whom she can identify struggling with their own problems, and if it gives insights to unfamiliar aspects of life, it will be a rich source of practical information.

Of course, television has its limits. It does little to encourage a young child to concentrate. The very medium seems to encourage a short attention span; it stimulates and entertains with short scenes and visual displays that change, long before a child is old enough to assimilate fully what is on the screen. For very young children television serves as a sophisticated mobile, a kaleidoscope of stimuli. The same can be said of cartoons where the manic action and fast music appeals to younger children.

Children can undoubtedly be upset by violence and brutality on the screen, and may certainly be misled by social stereotypes. But it doesn't follow that every child will be seriously led astray by what is seen on television: for that to happen two conditions have to exist. The first of these is that a television programme depicts events in a way that is misleading or potentially harmful: the second, which is just as significant, is whether television is the sole source of the child's knowledge about the topic in question, a state of affairs that will only occur if much of her viewing is solitary and her parents are not in the habit of talking to her about things seen on television. Fortunately, although there is not much we can do about condition one, parents can do a great deal to prevent the second. Through talking to their children about unfamiliar events and explaining things that are hard to understand, parents can make sure that they do not have to depend upon television alone as a source of information about the world outside home, school and family.

On the whole, it is much better for a child to watch television with a parent than alone; you can share your child's experience and make it possible for her to talk about it with you. Such discussions will give you some valuable insights into a child's world. Barbara Tizard and Martin Hughes found that when four year old girls who had been viewing television on their own were asked about what they had seen, the majority did not seem to have understood what they saw. But when parent and child watched television together, most parents provided plenty of useful information that helped their child to understand what was going on. Parents often pointed out interesting things, named letters, provided relevant background information, asked the children about what they were seeing, or drew attention to similarities between something seen on television and the child's own experience: 'We saw horses like that in the park with Daddy, remember?'. Here is one conversation in which a mother responds to her four year old's questions about a television puppet.

Child	**How do they make him talk?**
Mother	*They just talk . . . the man talks in a funny voice.*
Child	**Is he inside him?**
Mother	*No, he puts his hand inside, and then makes the puppet move, and then he talks.*
Child	**What?**
Mother	*He talks, and it sounds as though the puppet's talking.*

Things to do

Assessing how much television is being watched

If you are concerned about the amount of television your child is watching, there are several things you can do. First of all, take the time to quantify exactly how much is being watched and what is being seen. This initial assessment will give you some useful clues about your child's viewing. For example is the child watching for real enjoyment or does she sometimes watch television as a way of avoiding other activities?

If you are actually watching alongside your child it will be possible to see how much television is really being viewed, and how much is serving as a background accompaniment to other activities. Very often, children get into the habit of automatically turning on the television as company, and only watch intermittently while they busy themselves with their toys. Once it is on, it may not occur to a child to turn the television off. If parents are busy, television can be a substitute for the human company that is not available at the moment.

Making changes

In order to reduce the amount of television your child watches, it may be necessary to take a subtle approach, depending on the age of your child and the current pattern of viewing. You may also have to reassess how *you* use the television. Do you tend to have it on in the background, and keep it on during mealtimes? You may find that your child's viewing habits are closely influenced by your own.

Introducing more selective or more family-oriented viewing can be quite an effective way of limiting overall viewing. One approach is for parents and children to cooperate in selecting programmes to watch, either daily or on a weekly listing. The actual process may be a good way to encourage your child to participate in decision making. If you have more than one child a certain amount of negotiation may be necessary. Making selections from a written source will also show the value of reading – young children are often keen to discover when their favourite programmes are due.

It is a good idea to work together to produce a timetable that lists the days, times and channels on which favourite programmes appear. (Doing this together shows a preschooler how useful it is to know about days of the week and times of the day, as well as being able to read and write.) If the child feels that she has made a real contribution to the decisions, there is a good chance that she will be willing to abide by them when a disagreement arises.

Watching television together

Don't feel that you have to watch all the programmes your child enjoys, but as noted earlier, research has shown that it is definitely a good idea to watch together. Doing so stimulates conversation and it has been demonstrated that children gain more from watching educational programmes like *Playbus* and *Sesame Street* with an interested adult than from watching alone.

Some children's programmes have a policy of introducing simple things to make, typically linked to a child's experience. Researchers at Nottingham University found that the combined auditory and visual qualities of television instructions are easier for four to eight year olds to carry out than where instructions were provided via words or pictures alone.

When watching television together you are available to provide explanations, point things out and help a child see the funny side of things. You can encourage her to think about the events she sees, question the values of television characters, and draw attention to stereotyped ways in which people may be depicted. All this encourages the child to think about and react to the information that television makes available, rather than just passively absorbing it, and helps her learn to use television constructively.

Dealing with television violence

As Maire Messenger Davies points out in *Television is Good for Your Kids*, if decency and good manners are consistently practised at home it is unlikely that seeing violence on television will have enormously negative effects. But there is no doubt that a number of children's programmes are too arousing for some children. They may become over-stimulated, and are unable to watch certain programmes without wanting to act them out. As one parent reported:

I conveniently 'lost' the video we had of *Thundercats* because my four year old was playing it over and over, immersed in the story and acting it out all the time. This meant extreme levels of boisterousness around the sitting room, endless pretend confrontations with swords and exaggeratedly physical behaviour. That was all very well, but it was getting to be at the exclusion of anything else!

Although both the cartoon and the child's behaviour may not have involved anything particularly violent, it is easy to understand the parent's concern. The child seems to have been gaining an unrealistic view of things, with the heroic characters seen as omnipotent and physically invincible.

Why are these cartoons so attractive to a child? One possible explanation is that they enable a child (who normally feels rather powerless) to imagine what it is like to have complete control and limitless power. Fantasies about having power and doing things with it — including having one's horrible controlling parents at one's mercy — can be enjoyed within a 'safe' context. Up to a point this is relatively harmless: children are being stimulated to exercise their imaginations, although not in a way which parents might want to encourage.

Perhaps surprisingly, some modern cartoons such as *Thundercats* and *Defenders of the Earth* list psychologists in their credits. But even if it is reassuring to know that the content of such programmes has been monitored by experts, be aware that they were not checked by anyone who knows your own child as you do. There may well be occasions when it seems right to you to restrict or limit exposure to certain programmes, and in deciding whether to do so you will have to rely on your own common sense and your knowledge of your child.

Videos

Videos give families greater control over what they actually see on television and when they see it. Pre-recorded tapes can also help to introduce new experiences or complement existing interests. The fact that a programme or a film is constantly available can create problems, however, and you may have to introduce some firm guidelines.

You may not own a video camera, but it is possible to hire one, and it will give you and your children a lot of fun, besides stimulating an interest in the practical concerns of creating a video film. Adults may already be aware of how television programmes are actually produced but for a young child this process is likely to be completely unfamiliar.

13   Becoming More Independent

Paul, who is almost eleven, is a bright child, whose
parents have always done their best to give him plenty of
stimulation and encouragement, and have made him sharply
aware of the importance of doing well at school. He is well-
informed for his age, curious and has high ambitions.

Yet Paul is having problems that threaten to impede his
progress. He is at an age when he is expected to do some
homework, but he is not doing enough to keep up. He says
that he finds it impossible to study on his own. Like many
boys of his age he is not enthusiastic about being alone and
prefers spending time with his friends, but in Paul's case the
problem seems especially acute. When he is supposed to be
studying he finds it difficult to concentrate, and he spends
much of the time daydreaming. Paul's parents keep telling
him that he won't get on as well as he could unless he
studies properly, but his written work continues to be
disappointing.

Paul's difficulties illustrate the fact that as children move
into adolescence, educational progress increasingly depends
upon personal qualities. Intelligence alone is not enough; a
child also needs tenacity and a sense of responsibility. A
recent study by psychologist Mihaly Csikszentmihalyi sheds
some light on how things might have been going wrong for
Paul. Csikszentmihalyi has developed a technique to assess
how young people actually experience the various activities
that make up their daily lives. In his research, participants

are issued with a bleeper, which sounds at random times on ten occasions each day. When the bleeper sounds, the participants are required to make a note of what they are doing at the time, where, with whom, and how they feel about the activity.

Csikszentmihalyi also obtained details about the family backgrounds of the young people in his study. Some of the young people had families who provided a supportive and structured home environment, with the parents establishing clear rules and expectancies for family members. Others had parents who put a great deal of emphasis on providing stimulation and encouragement to learn. Some families provided children with one but not both of these features, whereas some of the young people had families that were both stimulating *and* supportive.

Csikszentmihalyi was interested in discovering how family backgrounds influence the ways in which children experienced the different daily activities they had been asked to record. He discovered, for instance, that when participants were asked how happy they were when involved in leisure activities such as watching television, or how strongly they were attending to the activity, most responded positively, irrespective of their family background. But when the young people were asked the same questions at times when they were expected to be studying on their own, responses differed sharply, and were related to particular family backgrounds. At these times, the majority of the participants reported that they were not feeling at all happy about studying on their own and were not alert or attentive to it. The only group of children who formed an exception were those who came from families that offered *both* an educationally stimulating environment *and* one that was structured and supportive.

It seems that this combination offers the best opportunities for a child to develop into an independent learner –

found in those who enjoy fulfilling lives, is only possible when an individual has a definite awareness of being relatively independent and in control.

This level of awareness does not just happen: a child must have opportunities to practise those skills that will eventually lead to a sense of independence. It is by doing and thinking for ourselves that we learn to act on our own, to make decisions for ourselves. Only by learning how to accept responsibilities does a child develop into a dependable adult. Young people who grow up in over-protective families where independent living skills are not learned can suffer real handicaps that plague them throughout life.

PROBLEMS THAT CAN ARISE

Sometimes parents who are especially caring and conscientious, keen to provide early educational experiences for their children, can find it particularly difficult to avoid overprotecting them. There are reports of child prodigies who were brilliant at science and mathematics but unable to look after themselves and stay clean and properly dressed without their mother's assistance. Often without knowing it, parents may act in ways that restrict a child's progress towards increasing self-sufficiency. There are a number of reasons why, the first being a natural wish to protect a child. We cannot help being aware that dangers exist, so it is not surprising if anxieties about them begin to dominate a parent's thoughts. All parents worry about their children, and the media never let us forget that no one is immune from illness, accidents, crime and disasters.

Naturally enough, some parents assume that the more protective they are, the safer their children will be. So cautious mothers and fathers do not allow eight year olds to cross the main road on their own, and some parents try to prevent their eighteen year olds from staying out late in the evenings. It is easy to see that the parents' reasonable desire to protect can easily restrict their child's progress towards self-sufficiency.

With young children, questions of simple convenience can impede a child's independence. When a baby's clumsy efforts to eat her meal result in a complete mess, or a parent watches her toddler struggling to get dressed, knowing that she is going to be late for work yet again, it is all too understandable that the parent will take the easy way out by helping the child. Doing so can save endless frustration, particularly when time and patience are limited. But it is important for parents to make sure that their child gets plenty of opportunities to learn the skills she needs.

Parents who identify closely with their children and are very keen for them to do well sometimes react negatively to increasing self-assertiveness, to signs that a child is becoming more independent. The difficulties can be particularly acute in families where there are special reasons behind this degree of identification: parents who are determined that their child should succeed where they themselves failed, or who are keen for their child to have opportunities they were deprived of, are particularly vulnerable here. Such parents may find themselves living their lives through their children, especially when a child's success is seen as a compensation for their own failure.

Families which are socially isolated or regard themselves as outsiders in the community where they live are especially likely to experience problems at this time. But for all parents it can be very painful when a child acts in ways that conflict with their own attitudes or values. Adolescents often make choices that are very different from those their parents would approve. They make friends with people whom their parents find 'unsuitable', and they often seem to take more account of the opinions of their peers than of their parents. Sometimes they reject plans for the future that, to the parents, seem to be self-evidently right.

For many young people, rejecting at least some of their parents' attitudes is a necessary part of becoming a person in their own right. Having their own tastes and preferences is a way of declaring their individuality. Family life so stifles some teenagers that they have to reject virtually everything their parents stand for before they can build an independent identity.

There are no easy solutions: we cannot live our children's lives for them. Our dreams are not their dreams. We cannot always prevent them from making mistakes, even when we see them coming. There are some things that a child can only learn by experience, however painful. Young people can be protected from some dangers, but they cannot always be protected from themselves. But children who have been encouraged from an early age to make their own decisions and have gained the habit of responsibility for their own actions, will be much better prepared than those who have not had the opportunity to learn how to look after themselves.

HELPING YOUR CHILD TO MAKE WISE DECISIONS

There is much that parents can do to help a child become capable of making sensible choices. By taking steps to encourage children of all ages to become as independent as their knowledge and understanding permits, we can help them to equip themselves with the survival skills they need. This does not mean that parents will never have to worry about their offspring, or that there will never be upsets during adolescence, and it certainly doesn't mean that children will end up always making choices their parents agree with. Yet children who are encouraged to act independently, to make decisions for themselves and take on responsibilities, are more likely to grow into mature and self-confident individuals who are capable of getting on with their lives.

Start young! Even the smallest children can be given lots of practice at doing things for themselves, making their own decisions and starting to take on responsibilities. As well as mastering everyday activities such as getting dressed and keeping clean, they can be encouraged to learn how to use the telephone, how to make purchases at a shop, how to plan their future activities, and how to cross the road safely. They can also learn to accept responsibilities, which may range from simple things like keeping toys tidy or helping to clean the house, to more difficult ones such as looking after (with parental assistance) the family's guinea pig or helping to take care of a kitten.

There are some traps that parents will need to avoid. Don't assume that either you *or* the child makes all the decisions. If you have to go to the shop it is just as inappropriate to say to your five year old 'Would you like to go to the shop now?', knowing that for practical reasons she will have to go anyway even if she refuses, as it is to say, without any warning 'Right, we are going to the shop now. Tidy up your toys and put your coat on.' It is more sensible to allow your child as much choice as is practical, but no more. You might say, for instance 'In five minutes we shall have to go to the shop because we need some butter. You can wear your blue coat or your grey coat. You decide,' or 'Tell me if you'd rather go by the road past the church or if you would sooner take the path that goes through the park'.

In both of these examples, the child is being given the opportunity to make a choice, but within firm guidelines set by the adult. It is important not to appear to be giving a wider degree of choice than is actually possible. If you tell your daughter that she can choose what to wear when she goes out to play in the park and she decides on her pink tutu, you have only yourself to blame for the consequences! Similarly, you will save yourself a lot of trouble by saying 'Would you like jelly or ice-cream?' rather than 'What do you want for pudding today?'. Young children who are accustomed to having most of their choices respected will accept that sometimes it is their mother or father who decides.

The capacity to take responsibility for others is something that has to be acquired gradually. Obviously you can't just give your six year old a puppy for Christmas and assume that she will be able to look after it, however often and loudly she has assured you that she can. Once she has already demonstrated her ability to look after a pet on her own, however, perhaps by regularly cleaning and feeding an animal for several months without too much help or nagging on your part, it will be safe to assume that she is prepared to take on a bigger responsibility.

As children get older the range of situations in which they can take decisions for themselves, act independently and assume responsibilities will naturally widen, and their desire to be in charge of their own lives will almost invariably lead to family arguments at times. Very few families avoid these conflicts altogether, if only because adolescents' longings for excitement, eagerness to take risks and willingness to experiment and act spontaneously are rarely shared by their parents, just as parents' inclinations to act cautiously and plan for the future are often not shared by their children. Safety and security are not high among young people's priorities, and up to a point, this is something which parents just have to accept. There are bound to be some issues on which you and your children will not see eye to eye. The important thing is to keep communicating, and not let disagreements poison family relationships.

One way in which parents can assist children to become

more mature, and perhaps more stable, is to help them with certain 'rites of passage' that signal the transition from childhood to the more autonomous position of the young adult. Having a paid part-time job is one example; an adolescent benefits from learning to take on responsibilities outside the home, having to organize time (and perhaps get out of bed at unsocial hours), and cooperating with adults who are not members of the family. A job also gives a person an important degree of financial independence. Learning to drive a car is another achievement which helps a young adult to be less dependent upon parents, and being able to prepare their own meals can also help to give young people adult status in their own eyes.

From time to time we read about teenagers who are wonderful tennis players, twelve year olds with first class degrees in mathematics, outstanding young musicians, adolescent grandmasters at chess, and others who strike us as being amazingly accomplished in their field. For some of these individuals their special skills will make it possible for them to enjoy careers that are unusually exciting, or fulfilling (and perhaps well-paid).

There is much to be said for the idea of encouraging a young person to become excellent at some activity, whatever it happens to be. As parents, we may occasionally wonder about the possibility of our own children becoming outstandingly able in one or other sphere. Perhaps we know a family or two where the parents have encouraged their child to excel at ballet dancing, or swimming, or instrumental music, or gymnastics, or football, or chess, or mathematics.

On the one hand, there is something rather worrying about parents who seem to be obsessed with their child's achievements – super-enthusiastic ballet mothers or tennis fathers often seem to be fulfilling needs of their own. But on the other hand there is a lot to be said for encouraging a child to strive for excellence. If we think it possible that a child of ours is capable of doing outstandingly well at an activity in which exceptional levels of performance will bring special rewards, should we deny her the necessary help and encouragement? It would seem churlish not to give all the support we can make available. Why not at least give the young person a chance to do something supremely well?

BECOMING A YOUNG MUSICIAN

What particular benefits does such a degree of specialization bring, and what probable costs and possible dangers are there? These are not questions that can be answered by a simple accounting process, because too much depends upon the particular circumstances of the people concerned. Along with two other researchers, John Sloboda and Jane Davidson, Michael Howe has been involved in an investigation of the early backgrounds of promising young musicians, talking to a substantial number of young people and to their parents as well. Each gave us some fascinating insights into an experience of childhoods where a considerable amount of time and energy was directed towards the training and practice needed to become a skilled performer. Many of the experiences of these young musicians and their parents are also relevant to other areas of specialization.

The youngest of the individuals we talked to were ten years old and the oldest were seventeen. All of them are unusually competent musicians for their age. At the time of the investigation they were studying at a specialized music school where there is considerable competition for admission, and the school only selects candidates who have already made excellent progress and are highly motivated. A number of the young people who talked to us had already had some success in national or local competitions or had been selected for prestigious junior orchestras.

Most of the questions we asked were about the years during which they first became seriously interested in becoming a musician. Predictably, none of the youngsters we talked to had lacked opportunities to learn about music and play an instrument, although slightly to our surprise only around half of the parents had a serious interest in music themselves. In every case either the family or the school had given the child better than average opportunities to learn an instrument. Although it may seem obvious that a child is unlikely to do well in music unless good opportunities to learn are made available, it is worth emphasizing that very few young children discover special areas of interest entirely on their own. It is also very unlikely that a child will do particularly well unless there is an adult who can give plenty of support and encouragement.

Parental help and support were found to be all-important for the successful young musicians, virtually all of whose parents were extremely supportive of their child's efforts. Our findings showed that in most cases, had the parents done less to help the child would never have reached the level of early achievement that is essential to attain a successful career in music. The idea that a talented child will succeed regardless of parental involvement is, sadly, not true. In most cases interviewed, not only did the parents take their child to the lesson; a quarter of them often stayed throughout the lesson, and over half had regular contact with the teacher to keep close tabs on their child's progress.

Similar evidence of high levels of parental involvement and support emerged when we asked what parents did while the child was practising. In most cases, rather than simply encouraging the child to go and practise, these parents played a much more active role. They were acutely aware that young children often find practising alone difficult, and took steps to provide the necessary support. A third of the parents supervised the child's practice in the early years on a moment by moment basis. Well over half of them gave frequent encouragement during practice sessions, and almost all of them made sure that the child kept at the instrument for an agreed daily practice period. In brief, these parents did not just leave things to the child and the music teacher, but assumed considerable responsibility for helping the child.

We also asked the young people what in their opinion would have happened had their parents been less supportive with regard to daily instrumental practice. In reply, less than one child in seven told us that they had been totally self-motivated, and would have kept practising without any parental encouragement. Even among these young people, whose early musical experiences have been remarkably successful, the vast majority freely admitted that they had depended on parental support to maintain a regular schedule of practising. A few confessed that without some parental pressure they probably would not have practised at all.

Music is unusual in the degree to which adult accomplishment depends upon training that has taken place in childhood, although research suggests that early encouragement is equally crucial in other fields. For instance, young adults who excel at tennis, chess, mathematics, ballet, swimming and diving, have almost always relied on parents who have been active and generous in providing time and assistance. Yet even the most strenuous efforts by parents is no guarantee that a child will succeed. Some of the most able young musicians in our investigation had siblings whose musical efforts had been just as conscientiously supported, but to little avail.

DECIDING TO SPECIALIZE

Both parent and child have to think hard before deciding to concentrate on a certain field, particularly where this may be at the expense of other interests. A child's progress and prospects need to be considered as objectively as possible. Does it seem likely that the eventual level of performance will justify the sacrifices involved and might a long-term career in that field be possible? How likely is it that injury may force a child to abandon the activity? Is it probable that the young person's interest will eventually diminish?

None of these questions can be answered in advance with any certainty, but parents owe it to a child to think about them as rationally as they possibly can. It is also important to be realistic about career opportunities.

Among young musicians, by way of illustration, there are numerous excellent pianists, many of whom would love to have a career as a concert pianist. The demand for concert pianists, however, is very small and only a tiny proportion of those who would like to make a living as a soloist will actually be able to do so. For the vast majority of young pianists, teaching will be the only career in which they will stand a realistic chance of making use of their hard-earned accomplishments.

The situation is not so very different in other fields: the number of professional footballers is tiny in relation to the number of would-be footballers, and remarkably few people make a living at chess, gymnastics, golf, or tennis.

It is unlikely that a child's specialized skills will help her to excel in other fields, even where unusual mental capacity is concerned. It has been remarked that the only reliable prediction that can be made about the abilities of a chess-master is that he or she is very good at chess. In other words, the fact that someone has acquired impressive chess skills does not provide any basis for knowing how well that person will do at other tasks or problems. Compared with someone else from the same social and educational background, an expert chess player is no more and no less likely to be unusually intelligent. Contrary to what many people believe, it seems that the mental abilities gained by someone who becomes accomplished in one particular area of expertise have little applicability to other areas of competence. In the case of our young musicians, for instance, there is no evidence to suppose that their being good at playing the violin or the clarinet will have any effect on their ability to do well in non-musical subjects – a fact appreciated at the school they attended. They all receive an education that will qualify them to study subjects other than music at university, if they decide that is what they want to do.

It is important, therefore, not to have unrealistic ideas about the extent to which a young person's accomplishments, may be relevant elsewhere. All the same, the experience of learning to do something outstandingly well does have broader repercussions. Put simply, it is good for a person to do well at something. Many of the young musicians we studied had gained real joy from their successes, which had also helped to generate self-confidence and self-assurance. They had also learned from experience that persistence and hard work are necessary if you want to reach a high standard of skill. The young musicians had also got into the very useful habit of studying hard and persevering with a hard task until it is mastered.

A number of our young musicians had clearly enjoyed identifying with their chosen field. Being able to think 'This activity is mine: this is what I can do well', seems to generate a sense of individual identity for a child. And for most of the older children in our study their interest in music permeated their lives and friendships; their interest in the musical world was far from narrowly vocational. They enjoyed a range of different musical activities, which provided social as well as musical rewards. Few of these young musicians had wildly optimistic notions of becoming professional soloists; more typically they envisaged a way of life which combined orchestral employment with, perhaps, some teaching and some playing in a smaller instrumental group.

In common with music, almost any area of specialization

brings its own unique rewards. All the same, it is never easy for parents to decide when, or how much, to encourage a child who has a strong desire to concentrate her energies in one particular direction, especially when that may mean restricting opportunities to experience other worthwhile activities. On the whole, however, the best advice to give to a young person who is really determined to excel at one particular activity or other is to 'go for it'. If the skills that are learned are ones that can be widely applied, so much the better.

Afterword

In today's competitive society it is hardly surprising that some parents are keen to push their child into being more successful than other children or smarter than the boy next door, but there are far better reasons for encouraging your child to learn. Whether or not we excel at any particular area of achievement, the kind of person each of us *is* depends to a large extent upon the learning experiences that have determined what we *know* and what we can *do*. For the young child, learning extends boundaries and makes all kinds of things possible, because newly gained knowledge and skills open doors into new experiences. The result is to make life richer and more interesting. At the same time learning helps make children more independent, because it gives them greater control over their lives.

Encouraging a child to learn is one of the most powerful ways in which parents can make a positive contribution to the child's life: a moderate amount of effort can produce a huge and enduring difference. Making that effort is largely a matter of taking advantage of the frequent opportunities for encouraging learning at home that arise in the course of daily life. The main goal of this book has been to give the practical help parents will require in order to make the best use of these opportunities.

Notes and References

Chapter 1   The research by Barbara Tizard and Martin Hughes on parents and children at home is described in B. Tizard and M. Hughes, *Young children learning: talking and thinking at home and at school* (London: Fontana, 1984).

Chapters 2 and 3   Much useful information about early development is provided in H.R. Schaffer, *Making decisions about children* (Oxford: Blackwell, 1990) and M. Schulman, *The passionate mind* (New York: The Free Press, 1991). Mary Ainsworth's research is reported in M.D.S. Ainsworth, S.M. Bell, and D.J. Stayton, 'Infant-mother attachment and social development: "socialisation" as a product of reciprocal responsiveness to signals,' pp. 99–136 in M.P.M. Richards, editor, *The integration of a child into a social world* (Cambridge: Cambridge University Press, 1974).

Chapters 4 and 5   Good accounts of early language development are provided by D. Crystal, *Listen to your child: a parent's guide to children's language* (London: Penguin, 1986) and M. Harris, *Language experience and early language development* (Hove: Erlbaum, 1992).

Chapters 6 to 8   Useful information and advice about reading to children and having conversations with them is provided in H.S. Wiener, *Talking with your child* (London: Penguin, 1988). The research into reading by Peter Bryant and Lynette Bradley is described in their book, *Children's reading problems* (Oxford: Blackwell, 1985). See also U. Goswami and P. Bryant, *Phonological skills and learning to read* (Hove: Erlbaum, 1990).

Chapter 10 A survey of research into motor development is provided in K.M. Haywood, *Life span motor development*, (Chicago: Human Kinetics Publishers, 1986). Evidence that in appropriate learning environments motor skill acquisition can be enhanced during the early childhood years is summarized in J.L. Haubsnstricker, and V.D. Seefeld, 'Acquisition of motor skills during childhood', pp. 42–102 in V. Seefeldt, editor, *Physical activity and well-being* (Virginia: American Alliance for Health, Physical Education and Dance, 1986).

Chapter 11 See M.J.A. Howe, *A teachers' guide to the psychology of learning* (Oxford: Blackwell, 1984).

Chapter 12 A good brief survey of the research is provided in P.M. Greenfield, *Mind and Media* (London: Fontana, 1984).

Chapter 13 For a comprehensive general survey of studies investigating the effects of early experience on later life, see M. Rutter and M. Rutter, *Developing minds: challenge and continuity across the life span* (London: Penguin, 1992).

Chapter 14 See M.J.A. Howe, *The origins of exceptional ability* (Oxford: Blackwell, 1990), and M.J.A. Howe, editor, *Encouraging the Development of Exceptional Skills and Talents* (Leicester: British Psychological Society, 1990).

Index